FEVER

Fever

Shilo Niziolek

Querencia Press, LLC
Chicago, Illinois

QUERENCIA PRESS

© Copyright 2022
Shilo Niziolek

LIBRARY OF CONGRESS CATALOGING-IN-PUBLICATION DATA

ISBN 979 8 9860788 9 2

www.querenciapress.com

First Published in 2022

Querencia Press, LLC
Chicago IL

Printed & Bound in the United States of America

"You are alone in Portland. You will never know the name of the tree whose bark is lime green. What am I to do with all of this unused desire?"

—Jay Ponteri, *Wedlocked*

Dedicated to all the girls and women who have loved someone they shouldn't.

Ectopic Rupture:

An ectopic pregnancy occurs when a fertilized egg grows outside of the uterus. These usually occur in the fallopian tube, and as the fertilized egg grows it ruptures the tube, causing major internal bleeding which can lead to death. The medical community refers to it as a spontaneous abortion.

Vulvar Vestibulitis:

A neuro-inflammatory condition in the vestibule, or opening of the vagina, in which inflammation starts from any number of a long list of reasons. This inflammation can cause severe pain during intercourse.

Even before there were cell phones that could take photos, I've always been the one running around taking pictures of the people I love living their lives. I have freezer bags full of the run-off from disposable cameras. My smartphone is filled with photos. They are eating up all of my data. The only pictures I've ever parted with were of a boy I loved. I chopped them into jagged pieces using the violent edges of scrapbooking scissors. I saved only one photo and it is hidden at the bottom of a box. I never pull it out to look at.

It turns out I don't need to. Nine and a half years since I left him, and he still visits me in my sleep as the boy I knew. Slicing up his pictures was, at the time, an act of self-preservation. Now I see I was compartmentalizing. I was practicing what would later become second nature to me. How to kaleidoscope a life.

I find myself fetishizing my own body: fresh from illness, tender and languid, thin, firm, and fermented. Feral. I've unfurled from the sickness that has plagued me into this new form, rebirthed, still with illness, but not dying, not curling around my body, not cradling my stomach, my intestines, not reading to remove myself from existence, but reading to feel. I don't want to have sex; I just want to imagine myself as someone who has sex. I see my body, for the first time, and again, as a woman's body. I twirl circles on the wood floor in my socks when no one is home. I walk from the bathroom, pants in hand, my underwear four sizes smaller than before, my breasts smaller, but no less desirous. I can witness the body as the appetizer, the body as full course meal, the body as dessert. I wear only lace bras that don't press in on the place that is home to illness.

My whole body is home to illness. In it, I am the queen. My body hasn't been a tool for sex in years. But inside my fresh body I feel eyes watching me. I feel my eyes looking out at the world, seeing eyes looking in at me. I wear a top with thin fabric. I feel suggestive. I want to be seen. I am following the line. I am casting out invisible nets. I am inquiring. I search it out, the falling. I reach for it inside my books. *Will you break my heart?* I ask of them. I put in movies that will make me cry. I see all the world. *Let me love you. I love all of you.* I live with them inside.

It's on the way to get waffles that my friend sparks in me an idea, telling me, "I have reconciled within myself that I am doomed to fall in love with everyone I meet."

Later at home the thought is still lingering. I think *If I write about desire maybe my words won't feel dry on my tongue.*

At night, I dreamt a woman with black spiraled hair asked me to call her. And later, I did. I tell my best friend, I dreamt of having sex with a woman last night.

What exists on the inside of the inside: what moves a person, what excites a person, what breaks a person, what has the ability to break a person? Who are you between the folds of your thoughts, in the creases of your heart?

A peer's voice fills the air in the classroom. I fall momentarily in love with this man who wrote about his voice turning to a quiver. When his voice quieted, as I have never heard it do, when he read from his own work about wanting "the one you love to be there beside you singing in the wilderness," I wanted to be the one beside him singing into the wilderness, into a storm. He played a recording of himself, from years ago, before the world stomped the song out of him, singing *Zueignung*, his eyes cast down to the floor as his voice fused through me. My eyes welled, and I was ripe. I imagined a small, simple apartment, somewhere high above a city. I imagined the rain beating down outside on the windowpanes, and him, bare chested, frying eggs in a kitchen in his bare feet, singing to himself. I imagined late in the night, my body entwined with his as he read aloud, one hand grasping the book, the other tracing the pages of my spine. Toward the end of his presentation he read, "Because I have no other way to tell you that I love you besides writing it into a speech that I will have to read in class," I imagined he was talking to me. My back, pressed up against a wall.

In *300 Arguments* Sarah Manguso writes that she only dreams about the people who she wanted to fuck but didn't or those she wished she had had more sex with. When I try to think of all the ones I didn't fuck or didn't fuck enough—I can't name them all. They are everyone. I want to line their bodies on a shelf: the unfucked, the not enough. I wonder what it's like to have a sexual body, not just a sexual being trapped inside an unsexual body. I wonder if she means she dreams about everyone. If I was the one who wrote that, that is what I would mean. I dream about all of them. I'm never not dreaming. Like Sarah I have desires that have formed grief inside my hunger. I keep the old hunger inside my body. I let it devour me. But then the grief comes from never knowing. An unknowing can be more painful than a knowing. Sarah writes that she is still haunted in mornings by a love's beauty. Is that what all this love is? All this half-formed, none-intentioned, never grown love is about? My boyfriend used to ask me, "You is loving me?" Almost eight years in, he has stopped asking. I save my love inside my body. I do not let it out. It spills onto the page. I pretend it didn't happen. My friend said, "Do you think he knows?" as we walked down a trail of green moss, green ivy, green trees towering overhead. I think so. I mean, how can he not? He was there; he saw. I was consumed by my first love. And when one of us speaks his name our bodies go tight, our shoulders tense. We become rigid, stiffened by things unspoken, unsaid.

A friend drew a heart to me on the corner of her notepad, mouthing, "You got this," in silent support. My professor told us about dreaming of a 15-year-old boy he saw who seemed sad, hunched, and moving slowly towards the school bus. He imagined different scenarios, different stories he told himself, about what was happening to the boy, what was happening inside the boy, to make him hold his body like that: scrunched and low. An older woman in a workshop read a prose poem about boxes inside of rusty boxes with windows that change and renew, and the poem gave me chills down my arms. Or was it the feeling in her voice, the way it rose and fell? My friend said, "You know how I curse people? I curse them by letting them curse themselves. Justice comes for them all. So, here is how I cursed my ex-husband." My professor said, "A couple years ago I stopped assigning Robert Walser books, because I love him so much. I love him so much that I couldn't bring him into the classroom." He said, "Write about one of your childhood hideouts. Write about the places where you go to hide, to find the edges of your body, to find out where your body ends."

My fourth-grade teacher lost her middle finger in an accident with a saw, and that was the finger she used to point at things: the board, words on the projector screen, her students. I remembered how fierce she was, her hair cut short, her eyes blazing with purpose. I remember her as old, but maybe she wasn't that old? Maybe I was just young?

I am rediscovering my body. I've been sick with autoimmune disorders for so long. I don't remember how to be a sexual being. I don't know how to be intimate, how to ask for intimacy, how to retrieve it. The lines of my body are new to me, yet they are the same. I have offered myself up before, to others, even to my partner of near eight years, *A*, but I no longer know who that girl was, or how. Now I am a woman, unfamiliar with a body, which has continued, and will continue, to betray her. Sex has been painful for years, due to a neuroinflammatory condition I have causing the friction to be more pain than pleasure. "What would happen if you told him you wanted to fuck?" a friend asked me. "I don't know. I wouldn't even know how to do that. How to begin." The words won't form in my mouth, and I can't decide if I even want them to form. Last night I was in bed next to *A*, our dog's warm body pressed between us. We were both on our phones, and I glanced to the side and really noticed him. Noticed *A*'s muscular arms, thought of the way they could so easily lift my desecrated body, toss me around, the way I used to love to be manhandled by my men, gripped roughly in desire. Then I rolled over, clicked off the lamp, and went to sleep.

As we prepared for the final and permanent closure of our beloved school on the Marylhurst campus, I couldn't help being swept away in awe, in a sort of rapture, falling in love with all the scribblers, the key bangers, the contemplators. I fell in love with their hearts, broken yet open, like mine.

I felt a sensual gratification while admiring the wedge boots that a woman wore. I don't even know her, but for a second, five seconds, maybe ten, I loved her. It has already left me. I've already moved on to my next great love. To the left of me, shoes shake rapidly on my friend's feet reminding me of a porcelain doll my sister and I shared while growing up. The matchbox girl. Made of glass, brown curled hair spilling out, rope around her neck. The image of her came alive, sitting next to me, standing on a cobbled street in London, the world covered in fog and soot.

On a drive home I fell in love with the orange-cream, frothy sunset clouds and the neon rainbow belting half the sky. The purple-gray sky coalesced, erupting into a downpour that I said a silent prayer for. I balanced my notebook on the wheel and steered with my forearms while the radio crooned, "I love the way you love me." And the window fogged up. And I could barely see five feet in front of me. And my hand cramped. And the sound of tires rolling through puddles vibrated through the window. And the moment was gone. And the dogs greeted me with affection when I stumbled out of a trance and through the front door.

On the way back to Portland from Ashland it was my turn to drive, and my two friends slept. I peeked at one friend from the corner of my eye; I checked on the other in the backseat. I was overwhelmed by such deep appreciation and gratitude that these women are in my life, that our friendship has carried us through seven years, going on eight. Before my eyes flashed a scene of us, many years later, our hair white and gray, driving somewhere, our friendship changed and grown. I imagined laughter inside that future car. I imagined tears. I imagined talking about the same things we talk about now: what is eating us from the inside out, what is piecing us back together.

It is blazing hot at my commencement ceremony. The professors begin walking down the path around the students. We break into an uproar. They make their way in front of the first line of chairs, where I am on the end. One of them opens her arms wide, her face, her smile, just as wide, just as loving. Another lifts a walking stick into the air, in triumph. HUZZAHHH, I imagine him thinking. On the back of their robes, in a silent protest against the school closing, they have pinned pieces of paper that read: *I am here for the students.* Our bodies press together under the ninety-degree sun, sweltering under our black robes. I fan my face. They announce that my professor will be giving the commencement speech. I see him standing to the side, behind the arborvitae. He wipes tears from his eyes. He steps onto the stage. He begins to speak. His chin quivers. "One student," he says, "at some point after she has entered the classroom, discovers in a moment she will not be able to exactly pinpoint in her memory but that exists as an instance of illumination, that not only does she belong in this academic setting, but comes to recognize within this space how her voice is distinctly singular while braiding with the voices of others around her, and these voices join the conversation about the condition of human nature." I am no longer fanning. The heat is unimportant. "For most of her adolescence one student has fought illness and decline in her young body, and now it's time for her to enter the classroom. One student loves crows and trees and books." He speaks, "One student realizes that writing cannot restore the female body, broken into parts, the body in decline, but she does realize that writing can regain the body, the words on the page become their own body, a body of text rising through the page's white space to your ears." He identifies us each. I can hear my peers. I see them as he speaks. I hear myself. I have been seen. We have all been seen. After the ceremony I ask to take a picture with him. After the photo is done, he says, "How could I not put a crow in that speech? How could a crow not just fly right down into that speech?"

The ocean is light. Did you know that? It illuminates the pitch of night, peels up the shadows. I bolted from a nightmare. Stepped barefoot onto the patio. The red glare of the digital clock showed 4:32. A woman walked her dog down the promenade. We let the world crash into us. With the door open I curled into a king size bed, dove back into sleep listening to a translucent lullaby of water crashing into the land. I awoke later, sand collected in the corners of my eyes. The birds cried out. I fell in love with a little girl outside my hotel window. She crouched in the sand, held out her arms and flapped them while thirty seagulls settled into the sand around her. For a moment, I fell in love with how I accidentally wrote crows instead of seagulls while writing this. I wanted to be that girl. Once, I was that girl. I wanted to remember being that girl. I wanted that girl to be my daughter.

I wanted to live on the beach, but only if it was the ocean of my past, and only if I lived alone, and only if I could wake up from nightmares to the sounds of waves crashing. Only if the dead of night became illuminated by the white thrashing silence of acquiescence, only if my new-old body could taste tender, salted clean. I'd run down the sand, and the seagulls would follow; the crows would loop above. The seagulls would swarm. They'd flap their wings in unison. I want to live on the beach, I think, but only if when the nightmares hit, I can step out of my worn body and into the sand.

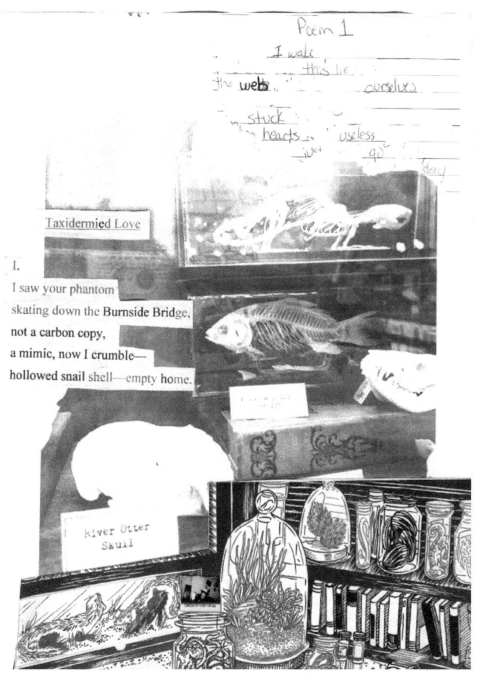

Poem 1

I wake
this lie
the **web** ourselves

stuck
hearts useless
just
go

stay

Taxidermied Love

I.
I saw your phantom
skating down the Burnside Bridge,
not a carbon copy,
a mimic, now I crumble—
hollowed snail shell—empty home.

River Otter
Skull

21

I used to spend months, years even, evaluating the decision to leave someone. Now, when I leave, I leave for good. No take-backs.

There should be a limit to how many times someone can break a heart. Pay the toll, girl.

I know enough about men to know that when they say, "I am a new man," what they mean is, *I am a desperate man.*

I dreamt I was in love with one of my friends. *Leave him*, she begged. My hands wrapped gently through her hair, her fevered kisses on my lips. *Leave him.* When I went, the lover I meant to leave was no longer there. In his place was an old love. He sat on the edge of the rocks of the Columbia River, fishing. Beside him was a pile of my things. *I thought about burning them,* he said. *I thought about burning all of them.* When I woke, I thought about messaging my friend. "I dreamt I loved you," I wanted to say.

After a year of renovating and reclaiming the original hardwood floors, it is finally complete—my writing room. A room of my own, a room with a view. Teal walls, shiny floors, four bookcases, a coral desk where I sit and rest my knee. From my chair I look up into the face of the gum tree. Sunshine glistens through the summertime branches, but I am already imagining the luxury of what it will feel like to sit here in the fall. I wish I had more to say. I wish I had time to say all of it.

It is only in the chorus of voices that I can understand myself. I am not singular. My desire is not my own. There is an inherit call and response that takes place when reading. It may feel silent, but there is a ricochet, a rioting in my heart.

While reading Sandra Cisneros short story, "Women Hollering Creek", about the legend of La Llorona who drowned her children in the river in a haze of her own darkness, I pause and stare out the window, imaging myself on the side of that lonely river with the weeping woman. *Here I am*, I say, the shape of the gum tree casting shadows on my pale cheeks. *Here I am. Thank you for coming. Thank you for coming for me.*

I am not singular.

I woke at dawn, the light dancing on the walls through the cream-colored curtains. The sun not quite up. "He is trying to do a sleep," *A* said. "Up. Up!" I said. Ragnar ran out of the room to the sliding back door, and I got up to let him out into the heat. I went back into the room. I shook *A*'s arm. "Up. Up!" I said. Curling up, climbing into a ball on my knees on top of him. Crushing him alive. His dry hands reached under my shirt. Rubbed me softly. I wriggled and laughed and tried to peel myself away. He clasped me in place. I unlatched myself and ran away. All day I have felt his lingering touch on my skin. Almost eight years, and I still can't figure out how to give us both the things we need. Is this self-preservation? Self-destruction? What kind of woman have I grown to be, who only dreams about bodies on bodies? Who writes about fever dreams and fantasies of love and fire and wants to be devoured by literature and memory and by the mud and the fog and the moss and the rain yet can't place her body in the hands of another person's body?

Is an abusive relationship a wrecking ball for all future relationships? Or was I just born this way?

Arundhati Roy describes a sun-wrinkled fisherman with secrets. The prose slithers, entwines, wraps around, converges, pulls apart, comes back together. I want to know this man. I want him to show me his sea-secrets. I shiver in the chill of it. And isn't that how we experience literature and books? We open the new page cautiously. We become urgent. The page a body. The body a page. The rest of the world, smoke. You shake your head, a dream. You are there under the monsoon sky. You feel the imprint. A ferocious rain comes bleeding down.

I came to the page today. Here it is. A bed made of creeping vines.

There was a young woman sitting outside in the blue folding chairs at the teahouse. She looked up as I was about to pass her. She wore a white tank-top and her hair was light brown. We made eye contact, the corner of her mouth lifted in a partial smile, a sort of *hello*. I turned to catch a glimpse of her, and I saw her slim shoulders dip around the corner. I said goodbye to her sun-kissed hair.

I am not getting any better at not falling in love with everyone I meet. The more the country falls apart the harder I want to love.

More than eight years ago my first love wrote, "I'll wait for you at the roundabout on the promenade. I'll wait there all day. Please come." I never showed. How long did he wait? Was there humiliation? A broken doorknob, too many times opened, too many times left unclosed. I wanted him to wait an eternity. I still do.

Last year, in a poetry class, we were required to pick a poem to memorize and recite. I knew right away what it would be: *Always*, by Pablo Neruda. He writes of a woman who calls hundreds of men to her, whose liquid body is made of the dead and drowned men she had wrung out. As I read it aloud, I feel myself, imperceptible to the human eye, raise my arms above my head, outstretched, as if waking the dead, as if parting the seas. The chills start in the center of my arm, shoot up into my shoulders, slither down my spine. My arms, they quake, and a storm rolls in. Purple swirls of clouds break around me and a hurricane awakens. I dance bare feet throbbing; my bare feet pounding.

What if we fall in love, not with a person, but with a thing? What if it is this great, big, brutal, magnificent world? My true love is books. I get to fall in love with everyone who has ever fallen in love, with everyone who has felt the stir of being alive.

A couple weeks ago I made a post on Facebook that said, I want my full-time job to be buying books. Is that a job? To which, of course, I really meant: Someone give me money to buy books for myself for a job. A professor from my community college days reached out and told me she had a friend who is a book buyer for a major bookstore, and would I like her to try and set up a job shadow. Yes! I replied. She forwarded the email between her and this book buyer that had a friend for a small independently owned bookstore who is also a book-buyer. The friend of my professor said: He's kind of a scatter-brained, romantic, youngish man who grew up in Portland. Super nice. I got the email while I was getting food with a friend and read her that line. I said to her, "That sounds like a man I could fall in love with." She said, "That's funny. When you read it, I thought, that sounds like a man Shilo could fall in love with."

I was talking to my niece about the gum tree in my front yard and the bright green gum balls that stab you in the foot if you dare to walk around in your front yard barefoot. I told her that in the winter they dry up and become hard and brown. She asked me which hurt worse, but I don't know. I don't have a measuring tape for pain.

My nephew is adamant that my mom's pumpkin plant, whose vines are creeping out of the garden, up over the rocks and up the stairs, may grow so big that it devours the whole house. Immediately, I wanted to set to work writing a short story about the pumpkin vine that overtakes a house, but I didn't do that. Sometimes, most times, I make a choice to let the things I could love pass me by. Instead, I sat with my feet propped in the sunshine, watching the honeybees take what they needed from the center of the flowers.

I'm not sure if it is apathy. Or if that is just the way he is. I often think about an Alice Hoffman quote about good men who are true but silent. And so I wonder, is that him? Is that *A*? Sipping tea with my mom in her sunroom, our knees curled and tucked into our bodies at the same angles, *A* sent me a picture of one of our dogs snuggled up next to him in bed. Love doesn't have to be passionate to be kind.

"You have to decide. Do you want a secure, but sometimes colorless life?" she said.

On any given day I am completely content, comfortable, and happy in my life and my relationship. On any given day I am two steps from the door.

A friend put out a request online for poems to read to her dying friend, to help carry her through the last leg. I immediately thought of Mary Oliver. That is who I would want whispering at my death march. An answer. An ode. A final fleeting sliver of mystery.

While sitting silently, tea clasped in one hand, my feet propped up on the outdoor table of my parent's front patio, there was a flitting, a flicker of movement to my right. Between the pumpkin vines and butter-yellow snapdragons stood a tiny little weasel swishing its long, brown tail. Its tiny feet rested on the patio. It showed its white belly and we looked at each other. A small piece of heaven, which is, after all, where we live.

I started working at a second-run movie theater. I was in the box office, taking tickets and reading *Eternal on the Water.* "We believe the world has become tired because it cannot sleep." It was the first rain in months. It covered the suffocating smell of wildfire smoke. I reached my hand out into the rain. I could just about hear the piano at the wine bar across the street. Just as I had to stop reading or start sobbing, a woman requested a ticket. She said, "Does that book take place in Maine? I think I was reading it on the plane one day, but I forgot it, and I haven't been able to remember the title." Her face lit up as I described the beginning to her.

I am not a goose. I will not wander the edges of the earth calling out the name of a lost love into a December sky.

A and I slept in a room on the beach with the patio door left open at night. Fires burned in little specks out in the sand. September chill crept inside the bodies' broken bones. My head enveloped by a cloud of dreams as he inched towards me on the bed, "Not tonight," I said, "Not tonight." My words slurred into sleep, "Talk to me about it tomorrow morning. Tomorrow." I awoke at 2:13 a.m. from a dream where we lay tucked inside the snow-white sheets, looking out towards the fires, now out, on the beach. It was the middle of the night, inside and outside the dream, and he moved below the sheets, my head above filled with the sounds of water. He said, "I love the way you make me feel," and in that moment I felt nothing. I awoke and the waves crashed outside. First thing in the morning he came over to my side of the king size bed, so large you do not have to touch each other at night while you dream about touching each other in a way you never touch each other. "It's tomorrow," he said. "Close the blinds so the people on the beach can't see," I said, despite myself. He closed the door too. The sound of the waves evaporated. It was morning, and it wasn't the middle of the night, and I wasn't caught in a fever dream. *The world is dry*, I thought, *and I do not feel. I do not feel. I want to feel good, but I do not. So, I pretend not to feel.*

All around you your heart is beating its rhythm in your chest, on your stomach, up against your body, up inside your body.

Vulvar Vestibulitis, they call it. An autoimmune disorder of the vagina. A neuro-inflammatory condition. The vagina says, "Help, I am in pain," and the bodies response is to cause more inflammation. *I hate you*, my body says. But I

33

wanted to love you. I wanted my body to be something that could give. I wanted a body that could take.

I haven't wanted to write any of this, but I may have already written it in an essay, or earlier in this draft, or somewhere else hidden, a notebook buried in a box of unfinished manuscripts. Some of the best sex I ever had was with my high school boyfriend, the one I lost my virginity to. Also, so was some of the worst. I remember fucking one night while he was high on oxy. The sex went on for hours. My body ached and trembled. I couldn't hold the weight of my own form up above his body anymore. I began crying. He couldn't finish from the drugs. They were prohibiting him from truly feeling. He was angry that I was crying. We kept at it until violently he shoved my body away. The last time we had sex, before I left him up on a logging road and drove away from him forever, we were staying at a friend's house. I had gone off the birth control patch which had been giving me blisters and boils on my skin. It was the 39th day of what I then believed to be the world's heaviest period. I thought it was from going off the patch. I was familiar with the sensation of paying for some sin I wasn't sure I had committed. We were having sex in the early morning. He slipped out and into my ass. I said, "No. No." he covered my mouth and continued fucking me, creating silence. The next day I left him on the logging road. That night I collapsed from my ruptured ectopic pregnancy. I know this is written somewhere else. The part about the death, the dying, the un-child, the end, the beginning. I will probably never be done writing about it. Some things you just don't move on from. You only get farther away. I will not talk to a therapist about this. I will not discuss what the destruction of a body feels like by the person you loved most.

I can't quite figure out how to write about the people who love me in all the right ways. The ones who want the best for me. I can only seem to write about broken things. But what of my mom? My glorious, enigmatic mom who is both loving and a thing that has been broken and rebuilt? Or my dad, who was really my stepdad, who adopted me, and who loved me as his own? Or my siblings, who I love so much I could burst at the seams from a shared moment of laughter with them as adults, or the numerable amazing friendships I've had over the years? Or my partner of over 8 years who isn't passionate or talkative on a deep or spiritual level but who makes me laugh on my sickest days. Where are their essays? Their books? I can't quantify good love. It's not unobtainable. There is no room for it in the pages of *Fever*. Or *Grief Distortion*. Or *I Was Crazy Too*. Nowhere in the mountains of drafts stacking up in my room.

Sometimes I go months without even a trace of desire for anyone. That doesn't mean my life is devoid of love. For instance, today, after three days of my lower back spasming, *A* put my socks on for me after my shower as I sat rigid on the couch with an icepack placed behind me.

Sometimes I think of calling my boyfriend back to the bedroom to fuck me, but I can't make myself do it. Am I afraid the mood will pass? That it's an act of trickery? It will hurt, as it so often does. Am I afraid I'll enjoy it? That I'll love him, more? In a different way? That my love will expand in places where I no longer want love to inhabit my body? "Goodnight," I say, "Goodnight."

My roommate said to me, "So much despair in one little body." I keep hearing it at random times, for days after. But, also, I keep thinking, *so much desire.*

In a dream I walk every day through a wooded area alongside a stream. I reach a small house on the edge of the water. Each day an old love and I walk along the riverbank. I find a note he has written on the inside of newspapers. *To Shilo*, it says. A cluster of cut out magazine letters glued to a newspaper clipping. Whole chunks and words of sentences have been removed, but the message remains the same. *I love.*

"What am I supposed to do with all this unused desire," keeps popping into my head. I start typing it in on google to see if it will tell me what it's from. Autofill kicks in. The options: what am I supposed to do with **my life**, what am I supposed to do with **this**, what am I supposed to do **without you**. When I do finally type in the entire sentence no quotes come up, but a list of things that PEOPLE ALSO ASK does: What are natural desires? What drives people's behavior? How do you bring passion back into a relationship? We are all walking around, vessels of desire just ready to erupt. Later, I learn the quote is from Jay Ponteri's book, *Wedlocked*, on the dissolution of his marriage, and I know why this refrain keeps playing.

In *Wedlocked*, Jay Ponteri wrote, "You deserve to understand what it feels like to love somebody enough you could die of it." I've loved somebody enough that I could die for it. In fact, I almost did, twice, but after my heart stopped on the rolling bed and again past the big white swinging doors, I lost the capacity to love someone so much that my knees would bend for them, that I would break for them. Has anyone loved me so much they could die for me? *Yes, of course*, I think, but then, *no, not now, not ever*. I'm hiding these things inside this work, burying them like a dog with a bone, only to present them to the world, at a distance. I want to be loved enough that someone could die for it. I want it to be you, beautiful strangers. I want the man I share my bed with to be the one who dies, who would die, who can't breathe for the mere suffocating desire for me. I want to be stripped bare right there, underneath a bright white moon and a world filled with trees.

The timeline actually isn't solid. Sometimes I loved. Sometimes I once loved. Sometimes I love still.

I stopped in the park and watched the crows flit across the sky. One flew down from a gum tree above me with such abandon that I could feel it beating in my body, ricocheting down my veins and into my toes. I felt serenely and incandescently alive. I found a crow at the curb, iridescent wings splayed, beak up against the black tar, dead leaves stuck to its wings. My stomach wrenched, but I couldn't look away. I wanted to lift the bird and hold it to my chest like a baby. I wanted to weep. I wanted to bring it to the crows in the park and apologize. I expected to dream about crows that night, but I dreamt of nothing.

A is a good man. We've been together for over 8 years. We have our dogs together and our house, and he is kind to me when I am not easy to be kind to. But sometimes I imagine what it would be like to meet someone and randomly fall in love and then just blow up my whole life.

There are no guarantees. I simply want to be with someone until our time runs out. If it doesn't run out 'til death, then okay, but if it does, that is okay too. I have no interest in marriage.

I dreamt that my partner and I were in a clawfoot bathtub. He kissed my collarbone but couldn't make love to me. He said it was because I want too much emotional commitment from him, that he couldn't be that person for me. I said, "If you can't, I am going to leave you one day." Sadly, he said, "I know" and then closed the bathroom door behind him.

I dreamt that *A* fell in love with a dying girl. He was devastated by her death when it came. Furious, I stomped around yelling at the friends of mine who had introduced them. "He was the only one who could treat her illness," they said, as if I weren't the dying girl.

A young version of one of my undergrad professors, whom I was sometimes secretly enamored with and who once kissed me while standing in the center of a crowd in a dream, came into the theater I work at the other day. He was flirting with me, or I imagined he was flirting with me. *What I wouldn't give*, I thought, as I scooped the popcorn. *What I couldn't give.*

On the phone with my mentor and friend I said, "I am working on this new project about desire." He said, "Amazing. I emailed you a link to a nonfiction book about desire." Immediately after getting off the phone, I ordered the book. I got online to read reviews and found people on there, telling their own stories of desire. Each person, reaching out in the dark, in the seat of a stranger's car. I don't even have the book yet, but already I am filled with its desire.

When a woman appeared at my door with a small gas can in hand asking for a ride to the gas station, I turned to my brother-in-law and asked him if he'd give her a ride. When he returned to the house, he said to me, "Never do that again. That woman was crazy. She didn't even have money for gas, and on the way back she tried to rub my shoulder. I told her I was married. She said, 'Can you touch me then?'" We laughed about it, but all day it sat with me. This woman, so desperate for touch, that in a three-minute car ride she would solicit it from a stranger as if it were a normal thing. Later, when my sister called me to discuss what happened we laughed about how ludicrous it seemed, like something out of a movie. Who was this woman? What was her story? *Can you touch me then?* As if it were that simple.

A woman who I met on Instagram sent me a private message. She wrote: *You were in my dream last night telling me how much you love your mom's hammock and that one day you want a love sack.* She attached a picture of a woman reading a book in an overlarge bean bag. I did not say that one night I dreamt we lay in her bed, bodies tangled around red cotton sheets, snow falling all around us in a room filled with windows. I touched the deer tattoo on her thigh, traced the lines of its flower crown. The snow fell through us, chilled our spines. Or maybe it wasn't the snow that chilled us, the feel of two bodies, unknown to one another, curled together in a love sack. I didn't write any of this. I wrote, *I love that dream.*

In the middle of the night, I dreamt that my ex and I had a hidden shed on the edge of a cliff that fell to a deep gorge where a river ran by. We kept our whole life in that secret place. A place where we could go to *be.*

I dreamt that I was back in Texas. An old friend and I made lists to rank the people we slept with. On a giant porch that seemed to stretch halfway through the desert she pointed to one of the men we used to work with and said, "I think I'll have you later for dinner." He turned to me and said, "What about you? Will you join us?" As we all stood up, I said, "No, I'm sorry I can't." When they left, I was walking toward the deep couch on the porch when a woman I didn't know arrived. "I would have slept with them," I said, "but I can't just blow up my life for anyone." She settled down next to me, "I know what you mean; if I returned to my ex's house even for a minute, I'd end up sleeping with him, getting pregnant, having his baby, and never leaving again." A small girl who hadn't been there before looked up at me, her hair a messy blond braid down her back, her eyes, a hazel like mine. I awoke to the sound of the wind outside thrashing through the cherry blossom tree, naked at the end of winter.

I awoke from a dream about the first man I lived with, the second man I'd loved. 5 o'clock in December, and the barely there light shone through empty branches outside the window. As for the man in Texas, I sometimes forget his last name, sometimes I forget him altogether, and he never visits me in my dreams. In this dream I was sixty. I said to a friend, "He always makes time to have sex with me, even now. He always makes me feel desired. That's why we last." *Did I love this one?* I thought I hadn't. I am pretty sure I didn't. I was still in love with someone else.

I awoke thinking: *I want to read a love story today. It's gotta be a love story.*

I said, "I can't imagine having to date again. I think back to my other relationships, and they were so exhausting because I constantly had to feel everything I already feel, which is so much all the time, plus I had to feel all their emotions too. And despite what I sometimes feel is missing from our relationship, with *A* I don't have to do that because he is so chill all the time. I can just feel what I feel, feel what all the people around me are feeling, but when I go home it's a safe space." My mom nodded, "Yeah, he is actually perfect for you. He is exactly what you need to ground you."

I've had two friendships with women that felt like romantic relationships. I was in constant contact with these women, always texting, calling, emailing, instant messaging, seeing them daily. One was when I was younger, and we shared a bed most nights, two bodies curled inches from each other. The other, in my adult life, separated by age and long-term partnerships with men. When they ended, they blew up fantastically. On a glorious summer day, wasted with the first friend and standing on the edge of the Alderbook pier we turned to see each other, our blond hair glistening in the sunlight. I don't remember who kissed who. It was the softest and sweetest kiss I'll ever remember. For a blinding moment the sunshine was eclipsed. When our friends noticed us, we were shocked out of our bodies, turned, and grabbed hands and catapulted into the murky Columbia River. Our toes touched down, sucked into the mud, before we pushed off and came up gasping. We never talked about it, and now that she is dead, we never will. After I ended the adult friendship with the other woman, she wrote a blog post about how toxic, emotionally abusive, selfish, and narcissistic I was and how much better off she is, and her marriage is, without me. I understand why she had to make me the villain, but a wound is still a wound.

In Katherine Angel's book on desire, *Unmastered*, she writes of hunger and the way she both shrunk herself and made her desire bigger to appease a previous lover. It's been ten years since the end of my first relationship. At the end, I bled for 40 days and 40 nights. And he didn't care. He wanted me anyways; he may have wanted me more, cut open like that. What does sex with a dying woman feel like? Power? I can't fathom a world where I would bleed myself dry for the love of a man, yet that world existed. It is this world. Like Katherine, I filled him with my unending desire,and he will never be free of me. 40 days of blood. I

44

stained him. Ruined him. Taught him that a woman should love him that much.

I think I'd like to take up painting. Now, that's a sensual art. The motion of the brush, the wet paint. I'd like to dump a bucket of paint over my naked body and see what that gets me. Fuck on a white canvas, one body red, the other blue.

Poem 2

You   addict

Taxidermied Love

II.

And what / if it was
you / the angles of your body /
scalpel / skinning knife.
In here / you are still / preserved /
mounted / papier-mâché heart.

I started dating the white knight after a violent fight with my first love, his best friend, who left the bruised imprint of 4 fingers on my upper arm. I'll probably dream about him tonight. He used to send me pictures of the ocean, of the dolphins that swam by his boat. He sent me a picture of a rock fish that looked like it was born inside out. Uglies on the outside. I was ugly on the inside. Sometimes I still am.

At a reading during a January New Hampshire storm, Jennifer Militello read about a boy she loved in high school who was no longer a boy, who no longer had blue eyes because he was no longer alive. I glanced down at my phone and saw a message from the twin of a dead boy with brown eyes that I'd loved. I opened the message to discover a picture of myself, hot pink stickered hearts around my head. I'M YOURS. BE MINE. Next to it was the envelope with the dead twins' name circled by a heart. His twin is in the Wyoming winter looking through the things he left when the cancer took him at 27, and I am sitting in a room of strangers on a side of the country I've never been to, experiencing the world. I thought about boys that will never be men and women who love men they shouldn't and girls who loved the right boy or the wrong boy or the boy down the street or the boy from the wrong side of the street or loved the right boy at the wrong time and then loved the wrong boy for a long time and I watched the freezing rain pelt down in the bubble of the street light and I only heard every couple of words that the person now reading at the microphone said.

For months I've been dreaming about snow. Not at night, but in daylight. *I want to be in deepest winter, I want to be in the desolate lands of Russia where the snow is six feet tall, or watching the artic fox dip through the dense forest of the Alaskan tundra, or up on Mt. Hood in the place where you might see a wolverine or a mink or a stark black raven calling out.* I can't stop thinking about the snow child. In a desperate attempt for something I want but can't have but don't want but might want but shouldn't have I'll leave a basket of snowdrop flowers out on my doorstep, or I'll build a snow child late at night while the flakes drift down in chunks and flurries, or I'll steal a child made of snow. I'll steal her, and I'll hide her away. She will be made of snowdrops and crystals and diamonds of winter, and she cannot cry, her body unwilling to break in those ways, and when summer comes, she will evaporate. And when the snow falls, she will come back. She will come to the door. She will rap on the wall. She will not need a coat. She will not need a mom. She will need only her one love, her winter love. The snow outside is glistening. I flew halfway across the country to see a river freeze below trees that look like smoke, and when I wake in the middle of the night, I stand at my window staring out at the dark while the white flakes catapult to the ground, building a pile, building a snow child, something that they couldn't have, something that they shouldn't have, delicate hands, and wet eyes, and a love that is not mine.

We moved inside from the cold and took seats in our heavy coats and knitted hats. The reading filled the air around us like a drawn-out piano note. In front of me, a woman rested her head on another woman's shoulder. Messy, brown, braided pigtails poked out of the end of one's black hat. The other reached out a hand and stroked the twists of the braid. The one with the braids didn't move. She didn't flinch. She didn't turn to give her a small half smile to acknowledge the moment, to assure her that this touch was okay. Minutes later she did it again. A human touch. An offering. A moment that my body can't quite absorb.

I spoke with a girl who lives across the country from me, stared into her freckles as she spoke of her younger sister who was bigger than life, whose name is tattooed on her wrist, whose person is contained in the ink, in the body, in the heart. I told her about my brother, my magnetic, devastating younger brother who, a month ago, said to me on a late-night phone call, when the world seemed like it was crashing down at his feet, "I think about death. I think about it all the time. Everyday. Multiple times a day." He said, "When I was in juvey, ten years ago, when you had your ectopic rupture, the guards came to the door and said, 'Your sister is in the hospital dying,' and then they walked away." He said, "Some days they'd tell me that I was being released, that our parents were coming to get me, that I needed to get my things ready and wait by the cell door. I'd stand at the door waiting, sometimes for hours, and eventually they'd come back. They'd laugh at me. 'Nobody is coming to get you,' they'd say." I looked out at the night. "Oh my god." I said, "Oh my god." The woman across the country said, "It's been ten years. I still can't write about her. I'm not ready."

In workshop, a woman curled on the couch in a sun beam and read aloud a Denise Levertov poem called *Intrusion*. I listened to her voice detail the cutting off of hands and the plucking out of eyes. Immediately, upon releasing the last word, she crumpled the printed page of the poem and threw it from her body. "Ah! I love it!"

A man who is exactly my type—red-blond hair, freckles, crystal blue eyes—read a poem he wrote on the fly the other day, and within the first three lines my eyes welled with tears. Today, when he hugged me goodbye, I didn't stand all the way up, and when we pulled away his arms grazed up my ribcage and across my breast. Hours later I feel it as an imprint on my bare skin.

A man who is exactly my type is at home in our bed with the dogs. We haven't *slept* together in three months, yet he is still kind to me. I call him to tell him I am short one hundred dollars while across the country, a miscommunication with the hotel staff, and could he please zap me the money. *Take care of me*, I repeat as he gives me a hard time, jokingly. "You is owing," he says, by which he means sexual fulfillment, and I imagine acquiescing, and I laugh as I deny his request. "Don't make me sleep out in the 4-degree snow," I say.

A man who is exactly my type once loved the love right out of my body. When we fucked, I felt like our bodies were one body and that without him inside me I'd never feel whole again. He once left me crying in the woods so violently I soiled my own pants.

I can travel 3,066 miles across the country, fall asleep looking at a different type of tree outside my window, the air so cold it could freeze the skin off your toes, and still when I sleep at night, I dream of you. In the dream you write me a letter and hand-deliver it and turn to say *I still love you*. I wake and the cold cuts through the blankets. Asleep again, I find us as teenagers. We are down at the riverbed, discovering tiny creatures inside the water, with each fish, newt, crawfish, brightly colored stone, your eyes light up with wonder and mischief. You pull each river creature from the water, place them delicately in my outstretched palm. I marvel alongside you, and after each blessing is released back to the water, I place my hands on you. A woman comes by and asks us a question, though I don't hear what it was. Your answer is simple. *He does not love what I love. He doesn't see the beauty in the world the way I do. He doesn't know the imprint of her hand.* I wake and the clock reads 5:30 a.m. and you are not here. I press my eyelids down on the fading image.

On my last New Hampshire winter morning, I lie in bed and watch the darkness quicken to a slight blue. A book of poetry, *My Love is a Dead Arctic Explorer* by Paige Ackerson-Kiely, rests in the crook of my arm and sucker punches me with lines about hunger and longing. I watch the silhouette of the trees become thicker with the ink of daylight. And yet, when I log onto social media, I see those I love doing things I love without me and I become envious of all the lives I'm not living in this moment, even though I return today to the kiss of my dogs, even though my head rests on a pillow made of feathers, even though today I will fly back through time, watch the world turn from dusk to daylight to night. I see them drink the tea I love without me. I see them walking on my beach, toes in my Pacific sand, sitting on logs that I love surrounded by my trees. I want to be everyone at the same time. I buy every book I can get my greedy little hands on. It is never enough.

My partner and I say *I love you*, but never *I miss you*.

Yesterday, though, he sent me a message that said, "There's a bunch of geese afoot."

One of my best friends didn't drink tea while I was out of town because she missed me and couldn't drink the tea without me.

I tossed for hours trying to fall asleep, my brain running rampant with ideas about moving across the country to New Hampshire, what feels like a country away, and falling in love with a person I want to write letters to, whose body on the last day of residency looked like a body a woman like me might make a home in.

That night I dreamt of having sex in public with my first love. I awoke at 3 am, the sensation of his hands still on me, my body already almost to climax.

I am watching a squirrel standing on the line of the fence, its face buried in my neighbor's sunflower, gorging itself on seeds. Yellow petals keep drifting to the ground as the flower shakes. My dogs want to go out and chase the creature away. *Let them be. Let one of us fill ourselves up with our own longing,* I think.

When my friend and I went to pick up her wedding gown there were two teenage girls trying on prom dresses. They danced around wildly on the lifted stage. I was sitting in a sea of mirrors, my friend in the dressing room making sure the dress fit. I felt old. After my friend came out, we sat in the sea of mirrors together and watched the young girls laugh. I said, "Ah, to be young and...young." And we laughed much harder than the girls, who turned and looked at us before going back into their dressing rooms, laughed.

Dancing for pleasure is instinctual, it follows the slow snake of the body. In eighth grade, my body freshly filled out into a woman's body, I'd dance in front of my mirror for hours, watching my body slither, I'd slink down onto the floor. There is a fluidity to dancing that can be matched only by the act of sex. Dancing, and sex, they are an impulse that begin in the blood stream, pump, pump, pumping. I felt this itch, something I haven't felt in quite some time, to move my body to music, rise up inside of me during summer residency at the pub, when all the brave and the drunk around me followed their desire, shuffled their feet, embraced their bodies as creatures of extension. The flight rattled around in my body as I watched them move. I swayed in my seat. I moved my feet. Finally, flushed I flung myself up beside them. I danced. Immediately, my heart began to pound wildly in my chest, my temperature leapt up, heat filtered into my cheeks. I became breathless. Afterwards, I bid everyone good night, tired in my moment of abandon. I stepped outside into the view of the New Hampshire moon. I laid out on the sidewalk, slowing my thrumming pulse, wondering how long it had been since I had laid flat on my back marveling at the stars and the moon.

I was telling a man I just met about the crow named Moses from *Mink River* by Brian Doyle. "The crow was injured and found and raised by a nun. She taught him to talk and read," I said. The man pointed to a tree and averted my attention to the only crow I saw during my whole week in New Hampshire. I thought of the thousands of crows waiting for me at home, careening from the towering trees, hundreds flying and calling all at once. "Hello, silly bird. What are you doing here? Go home?" By which I meant, *Did you follow me here? We are two crows, out in a world that we do and don't belong in.*

Once I found myself loving a boy who thought that everything was a tooth and nail fight, who thought that bleeding for love was the only way to love. "You're so pure, like a flower," he once said to me. Later, he would say, "You don't even know who you are. You have nothing to believe in. You live in a fantasy world. The world isn't rainbows." But he was wrong. I knew what to believe in all along. What I worship is the whole god damned miraculous world. Even a man who would say, "I love you," in the same breath as "I never want to see you again." Isn't there space for both? Isn't that one of the fucking beauties of being alive. We can hold two polarized ideas inside our body. I once loved a boy who was a euphoric, dynamic, loving, charismatic, controlling, imbalanced, mentally unstable, abusive mess. Once upon a time the world was not black-and-white.

In *The Uses of Sorrow*, a poem that Mary Oliver dreamt up, she wrote about loving someone who was darkness, and sometimes when I wake from dreams of my ex that refrain plays in my head like an 8-track stuck on repeat. I don't want to say the things he did to me were okay, because they weren't, but loving someone the way I loved him, all wrong even when it felt right, well, my god, the things I learned.

I met a girl in the bathroom in downtown Portland with long curled blond hair in a maroon dress with adorable boots and when she saw me her face erupted into a smile and she spoke about visiting Portland for the first time, and before I knew it, we were standing in the hallway between two stores. She told me all about the sweet homeless man she had met earlier with the best-behaved pit bull she had ever seen and we talked for five minutes about our pit bulls. I told her that I was going to do a reading that night for a writer I had loved who had passed away, and she said, "That sounds like it is right out of Gossip Girl," to which I laughed, to which she laughed, and when we parted she gave me one of the most sincere hugs goodbye I have ever received, and I walked back to the bakery and told my friends about the magic girl from the bathroom and we stepped outside into the sprinkling rain and a brick church steeple stared down at us with its stained glass windows sparkling, and I thought: *What do you really know about the world?*

I read an essay of Brian Doyle's out loud to a small intimate crowd of people who personally knew Brian: his wife who read an essay of his before me, his father who read an essay of his after me, his colleagues, his friends, my old mentor who read after me, the Oregon Poet Laureate who topped us off, sent us careening down into our Brian Doyle caves. They allowed me to be a part of the end that is not the end of the story of Brian Doyle, which is an endless story, an ongoing story, a story deep and illuminating and exquisite. We all must return to the earth which we walk on, lay down on, forget about, remember. The day Brian Doyle passed away I was at my sister's thirtieth birthday party. I tried not to cry at the party. On the 45-minute drive home I cried on and off in the car. I didn't know Brian Doyle. I did not know this man with a kind and sincere heart and with words that flowed down and around like the Columbia River we shared, side by side, separately. "I feel completely unqualified to be here." I said to these smiling-grieving hearts at his reading, "I came across this essay at a time when my university was closing, and I was making my way through a yearlong battle with illness, and this essay reminded me to look for wonder in all the small spaces."

My partner and I were discussing the spider plant looming on top of the dresser, dried out limbs needing ripped out. "I couldn't remember the last time we watered the thing, so I gave it a couple cups," I said. "It's fine," he said, "Look, it even has new buds." I lifted a branch, "That thing just refuses to die." That night, I dreamt that a spider plant was growing out of my ankle. The green sprouts wound around my calf, looped up the side. I could see the root system under the sheer layer of skin. I plucked the new growth out. Weeks later I put the spider plant outside on a sunny day, mid-rainy season. I forgot to bring it in before the rain started back up. Then, I just didn't bring it back in. This went on for months, and now there isn't even a twig left of its leafy branches in the whole container.

I am sick of affirmation poetry. Why do we all need permission to be human? You aren't always going to be kind. You aren't always going to do the right thing or think the right thing or be a good person. We aren't traveling down a scenic road that has no stops, and even if we were the scenes are getting bleak, the water is drying up, the animals have gone into hiding—but where?—there are no trees left to duck under.

I feel as though I am shuffling a pile of garbage from one place to the other. In the literal sense, I am doing this in my messy house. Writing, reading, cleaning, working, everything feels like a vacuum, and I am a twig, small enough to go down the tube, but turned sideways, lodged. I feel the force of the propelling air with no actual movement.

After I dropped out of high school, during a space where me and my on-again-off-again boyfriend were off again, I tried to hook up with a boy while we were high on pain pills. He couldn't get hard enough to fuck, and I got up, put my sweatpants back on, and went to bed. Two days later my boyfriend and I were on again. He told me that he ran into the other boy who boldly said, "I tried to sleep with Shilo." He said, "Yeah, it didn't work." My ex laughed in his face. Recalling this moment, over ten years later, I get the sensation of butterflies in my stomach.

The lunar eclipse came, and we stood outside on the back patio breathing frost clouds into the night. *A* stood behind me, arms wrapped around my shoulders, pretending to be sweet while rubbing his body against mine. He pretended to howl when the moon disappeared. I did howl. The neighbor's dogs and our dog, which had been silent like all the animals become when the world momentarily blots out, ran to their fence lines and began barking. All of us wild in unison. The moon appeared again. *A* went to get our wolfdog away from snarling at the little white wolfdog across the way who was snarling at our wolfdog through the metal fencing. I came back inside laughing just as the one lone frog I've been hearing late at night awoke from its momentary slumber.

I get goosebumps shivering up and down my spine. The back door is open and spring birds, which never really leave because it is almost always spring in the rainforest of the Pacific Northwest, call their throaty songs for those who will listen, and I can't help wondering who I would be if I hadn't figured out how to love both what I can't have and what I can.

On the morning of Mary Oliver's passing, I spent the hushed quiet revisiting one of my favorite poetry collections, *A Thousand Mornings*, which is every morning. Her voice rang like a chorus starting at dawn that day; it filtered around us on social media, in news outlets, sitting heavily in our minds like the birds who perform the magical migration dance, swirling up into the sky. She is the second writer whose passing has made me cry. But as her words vibrated around us through the entirety of the day, and I flipped slowly through the pages of her poetry, I was reminded of mystery and magic and the experience of letting things go in my favorite of her poems, *An Old Story*, about waking in the middle of the night that smells like spring and finding her body pulling her outside. Sometimes I am dragged by sensation in this way, pulled toward the strawberry super moon hanging pink and daring over the cedarwoods stretching in the sky. It is hunger I feel then, always that indomitable force of my body's cravings leading me into the dark.

In a dream I had, scientists found a way for men to be incubators for babies. *A* was full term pregnant with our children and a witch doctor took him to a back room to cut him open. He placed first one newborn child in my arm, then another. Twins, I looked up in awe for the children I was never supposed to have, their mouths puckered in a tight fist, ready to scream. I shifted the babies in my arms and noticed wires coming out of their backs, hands made of rubber, fake synchronized cries leached from their budding mouths. I gasped and dropped the fake children. *A*'s body lay behind the curtain, unmoving.

A friend ran into her ex the other night at a bar. He tried to speak to her, and she told him she had nothing to say. *Way to tell him to fuck off politely*, I typed. *I wish I could have*, she wrote, *but my heart was pounding the whole time and deep down I wanted to hear what he had to say, but it's pointless, so I took that route and hopefully I won't see him again for a long time.*

I recall the shape of my high school boyfriends body walking out of the woods, the way his shoulders always stretched out, raised, proud. He is walking out of the woods after smoking bowls with a group of people. He is walking across the street to talk to a female cop who only graduated a year before, who used to smoke weed in this same spot, with these same people. He leans into her car, stoned, laughs with her. She smiles like she is the tallest brightest sunflower in a field of tall, blond, beautiful sunflowers. She drives away. I am not sure why this is important.

What am I supposed to do with all this unused desire? I see something. I walk past. Forgotten. I see something. I put it down on paper. Where is the line that I must cross? I used to write our initials in the sand. Even the black sand at the river beach. I still don't know where the line of you ended and I began.

Taxidermied Love

III.
The dreams coming in
March of you, each like a flip
book, going, gone. You
belong in December dreams
icy blue, frozen til the thaw.

Poem 3

I'm frozen

look at me

66

I told my partner that I am working on a book about desire. I told him that it is about all people: my desire to be with people, to experience them, to experience the world through their eyes, my experience of people, of being a person in a body. "If this book gets published, will you leave me?" He shrugged, "Maybe," he laughed.

What am I asking of me?

After reading *The Seas* by Samantha Hunt, I searched
through my sticky notes looking for clarity, for
understanding of this strange and terrifying dream. The
content drags me out from under the slam of an invisible
wave, tormenting me with the possibility of starving loves.
But all I understand is I want more of this, more of this
spiraling grief and this utter confusion and this violent
understanding of a woman who is on the verge of
everything all at once. In a dream I create my ex-lovers.
When I wake from fucking them, it is like I have really been
fucked. The sticky notes tell me nothing. One sticky note
reads: *This book is so beautiful I want to peel out the pages
and staple them to my wall.* Another quotes the book, all it
says is, "The street is dreaming," What was I trying to say to
myself about the things I don't understand? Another says
the word *Disassociation*, while another yet is blank. "He
whispers very quietly, losing more of my clothes. There and
there and there. I have never felt love in my lungs before." I
feel a throbbing, a thumping, a pounding in the crease of my
jeans. Words are masturbatory. "...there is a foreign feeling
in my veins, it is the feeling of finally getting what I wanted,
and the feeling is colder than I ever thought it would be.
The feeling won't let me sleep."

I had to fondle fern feathers and listen to a robin sing at the top of a mighty naked tree and tell me the story of spring. I had to rub rock moss at the tips of my fingers and watch dusk crease over the edge of a field of tall dry grass and imagine cougars and witches and cabins in the middle of nowhere. I had to read three poems while sitting on a stone. Exactly three. And when I had to leave nature, when I had to set my feet first into grass, then gravel, then paved road, then to the peddle of an unwilling vehicle I had to listen to *The Sound of Silence* on repeat.

I dreamt that I visited Wyoming, and me and my middle school best friend, fell asleep in a rabbit hollow of a giant tree that was filled with snow. I woke inside the dream after dark, and in the light of the snow noticed small bluebird-colored, porcelain child hands buried. I excavated them and woke her. We climbed from the tree into a night of winter thick with a fresh dense layer of snow. We walked down where a road had been in a sort of daze when a hunched and frightening man came around the bend. "What are you girls doing in my tree?!" I handed him the tiny hand, while blocking him from her gaze and woke up terrified in my bed, in an Oregon winter where no snow was on the ground and the barren trees' silhouette watched me through the dark window.

I stepped out into the cool January air in my bare feet, pressed my toes into the squishy green moss-grass of our yard. The tips of the rose bush stalk had small buds peeking out and I felt them bloom inside my chest. Iris bulbs pressed out of a clump of dead leaves I haven't found the time to clean up, and the wind whistled around me, danced with the shirt on my back and the undried hair at the top of my spine. A crow called into me from down the street. The dogs laid on the couch in the sun, blinking their eyes in almost sleep.

A couple months into dating my high school boyfriend, he was sent to juvenile detention for a probation violation. I sent him letters daily, checked the mailbox each day looking for a reply. I can't remember what my mom thought, what her reaction was. All I remember is longing. The ridiculous longing of a sixteen-year-old girl. In later years, when he was locked up again, I remember a phone call with his mother. "He needs help. He isn't right. He always gets so angry, so violent. I don't know what to do for him. He refuses to see a therapist. You should take care of yourself."

In high school my bedroom was in the basement. I would hoist myself up into the driveway, crawl on my hands and knees until I hit the sidewalk, sprint all the way to his house across from the graveyard, ducking behind cars or bushes whenever I saw headlights. My boyfriend had a bedroom out in the garage which his stepdad had turned into a little apartment. He had his own bathroom, kitchen, and living space. He slept on the leather couch instead of a bed. We'd stay up all night having sex on that couch. Sometimes we'd start having sex in our sleep, only to wake up, bodies entangled, sticking to the sheen of the leather, already halfway into ecstasy. One day, after he hadn't answered my calls for two days, my best friend drove me to his house. She waited outside. His parents weren't home. I could hear him inside with his ex-girlfriend. I yelled that they better open the fucking door. I was on my way to a soccer game and had my cleats on. I kicked the center of the door so hard that I could see the door separate from the frame, leaving a gap in which I saw her face sitting on his couch in the dark, eyes like saucers, before he slammed his body against the door to keep it closed. Years later, sitting in my car across from the graveyard, he was upset, angry about something again. He punched the heater vents in the hood

71

of my car, and they popped out of their sockets. His knuckles immediately began swelling, aggravating old injuries. When he began to cry and apologize, I said, "It's okay. It's okay. Look, they just pop right back in. It's not a big deal." I kissed him goodbye.

At Eternity's Gate, the biopic about Vincent Van Gogh, is an experience in beauty and madness. Like Willem Dafoe I need a fevered state. I need to experience the world fast and slow. It is the same way I need to experience art making and love making. Chaotic. I need to be out of control. It is a fevered state or nothing. A violent storm or abyss.

I dreamt about a woman I don't know. I dreamt about her body, naked, her nipples raised. I dreamt of our bodies together in motion. We were in a cabin. I remembered having been there before. There was a crack in the sky where the snow was getting in and icicles were dripping, frozen, down the inside of the log wall. I stood in a wool blanket afterwards, the scratchy material up against my raw skin. *It is beautiful*, I said to her, turning to see her dark, silky hair spread across white sheets. *Beautiful isn't an adequate word for what it is*, she said.

A half-white fawn used to roam the hillside of our coastal town. I can see her perfectly, the contrast of her purity up against the wall of fog surrounding the dark green of the trees. When I think about her, I am always surprised that I don't dream about her. You'd think that a deer made of snow would appear in the dream world. You'd think I'd dream of something like that every night.

It is February. We are having our first snow. I've been waiting for it all day. The anticipation of falling white clouds has permeated the day, but each time I look up it's been rain, always rain. Then, a glance up from the pages of a book, white flakes fall from the grey sky, land in the vibrant green grass. Evaporate upon contact. I walk to the window. *Just like love, gone as soon as it lands.*

I keep thinking of this work being published and think of my partner leaving me afterwards. There is both fear in this idea and elation. My body craves destruction. Maybe that is why I am plagued by illness. I feel stiff, as if I have lived in the luxury of comfort or complacency for too long.

I slept with a boy a few years younger than me for a couple weeks. This one was during an in-between space where my high school boyfriend had left me to pursue vaginas he could feel untethered to. Uncomplicated legs split open. I remember, just after fucking one day, he was texting a mutual friend, both of ours, and of my ex's, who said, "You're with Shilo, aren't you?" I remember taking his phone and sending a reply, talking about how good I was. When we got a reply, I don't remember what it said, but I remember the sensation, the realization, that my ex was on the end of this other boy's phone. I felt a wild sensual power that was mixed with terror. I don't remember ever talking to my ex about that boy after we got back together, but I do remember running into the boy while I was with him, the way his jaw tightened, as if zipped up to his earlobes. I felt a thrill then. I feel it now. Years later, I ran into the boy with my current partner. His jaw tightened in the same way. He made some derogatory comment about him afterwards; it appears he had also slept with my partner's high school girlfriend while they were together. I turned from him, and my lips twisted into a smile.

I like to imagine that when I run into the men I have slept with that they see me as I was while fucking them, in the moments where I was my actual self, a wild sexual being, liberated by the act of sex, free from the bounds of my societal skin.

I am simultaneously sure that *A* is good for me and that we should be together, while also feeling a blade inside me that seeks to sever this connection. I want so badly sometimes to be cruel, to cut like a knife, to fall in love again with someone who is all wrong for me, yet makes it feel all right.

On a porch under the giant Texas sky smoking a cigarette an old work friend said, "Shilo chooses bad boys 'cause she wants to fix them." Another friend, a man in his forties, turned to look at me and laughed a little. "No, she doesn't," he said, "She picks them because she knows they will give her a reason to leave." I took a drag off my smoke. Never since then have I felt so seen.

Walking our dogs through the park the other day we came upon a flock of crows gathered around the edge of a pond, some sticking to the branches of a nearby tree, most on the edge, a few others up to the base of their bodies in rainwater. "The crows having their daily congregation," my partner said. One day while driving over the Glenn-Jackson Bridge, Mt. Hood stood, snow-capped and stately over the Columbia River and the silhouettes of the forest reflected in the sunset on the water. I said, "Look at it! It is magnificent!" And he said, "Looks the same as every day." And the bones in my body shook violently under my skin, and the rest of the drive I thought, *Who are you?*

There was a week in high school where the friends of my boyfriend's pregnant girlfriend called my phone and sent text messages to me daily. They were nasty. They wanted me to die. That was what they said. One day I was upstairs in the projection room at the movie theater I worked at. It was the end of the week of messages. A girl called me. She had been the main instigator, the main attacker, the main enforcer of some law they were living by that said this person gets to love this boy but that one doesn't. I answered the phone this time. She began to lay into me. It was after I had dropped out of high school. I couldn't bear to see the girl's giant full belly roaming the halls. It felt like she was waving a trophy in my face. The girl said, "What kind of weak ass bitch drops out of high school because she can't handle it emotionally—" I cut her off. "Do you have any idea what it feels like waking up every day wanting to die!" I don't remember what else I said. I remember she stopped talking. I chucked the flip-phone across the room and it catapulted down the stairs and broke into pieces. She never called again. I don't remember feeling like this. I don't remember wanting so badly to die. But I do remember, another time, in the pouring rain, driving at least twenty miles over the speed limit on the winding back roads, coming up to a sharp corner and thinking how easy it would be to just plunge over the edge and into the bay. Years later, after returning from my year in Texas, I started hanging out with a new group of friends. The girl who had called was in this group. Months after hanging out, I told her I remembered what she did to me. I remembered the calls. Her face was blank, lost, "I'm sorry, Shilo," she said sincerely. "I don't remember doing that." I looked down at my hands, looked up. "Well, I just want you to know, that I remember. You seem different now, and I am glad we are friends. But you need to know that I remember."

One night in high school my friends and I took two cars over to Never-Never-Land, a cove on the other side of the Megler Bridge. The Megler Bridge is a giant, green bridge that curves its way down into the hillside scape of Astoria Oregon, and in the other direction shoots up into the air before following a straight path to the Washington side of the world. We took two cars, and everyone was drunk or on their way. At the top peak of the bridge, we parked and hopped from the car. There was no one else on that stretch for miles, just us and the darkness and the fog that hid our home and the view across the bridge from us. We ran circles around the cars, laughing hysterically, as if we were getting away with something, as if we were not reckless at the peak, at the place where people come to jump down, down into the frigid waters of the Columbia River or down, down into the parking lot of the Holiday Inn Express. We hopped back in our cars and sailed into the fog, water on both sides, black and creeping and ready for us should we wish to return to that sort of home.

I've been thinking about the way we grow old. About the loss of something, the loss of everything, while also changing, shifting, gaining. A friend from elementary school posted a picture of herself in a bathing suit. She said something about her having lost her ability to see herself as sexy or desirous. She has lost the intimacy of being intimate with her own body. I too, have lost this thing, this instrumental piece of who I was my whole life. I don't remember a time, even young, when I wasn't aware of my body as a sexual thing, a writhing thing, a seeking missile. The same thing happened to me, and I can't exactly pinpoint when it did. I'm currently trying to write my way around desire and how I used to be a sexual being, so comfortable and sure of my body and how at some point it changed. I'm not sure if it is helping, but some days I think it is a little. I want to remember what it was like to feel vibrant in my own body. Is this something that is normal for our age? Both of us are about to cross the threshold of thirty within the next year. Will we appear on the other side suddenly in love with the construction of our bodies? We will remember who we were as teenage girls? All swinging hips and crushed red lips.

The way I took control back over my own body was to not allow the body to do any of the things it used to love. Sports were the first to go. Goodbye, running. Goodbye the feel of the wind rippling my hair out behind me. Then, I got rid of the drugs and the drinking. I don't want to forget. I want to remember forever into eternity. I never want to be done experiencing my past. It was fucked up. It was beautiful. It is all mine. Then, the body said, be rid of sex, throw it from your body, violently. I wonder what A thinks about the girl he originally started dating. The one who, drunk, at the local bar said brazenly to him, "I'm out penis hunting!" Who then, weeks later, began fucking him daily, wherever she could, most often in the front seat of his Mazda truck, behind his parent's house or on logging roads or dead-end streets, the trees always towering down at us. Does he think, where is that girl? *Where is she?*

Following the online trend in which we show an image of ourselves from the beginning of the decade verses the end I am struck by how much has changed, not just physically, though there is a decent change there. At the beginning of 2010 I had just recovered from my ruptured ectopic pregnancy. In the image taken of me, my hair is the longest it's ever been, my face narrow, and underneath the clothes I was wearing there are still deep black and blue bruises that line my thighs, vagina, and hips. Thinking back on the night of the image, I remember an old friend was very drunk and got up in my face. I was sober, as I was only months sober from an abusive relationship and a prescription opiate addiction. I do not know what this old friend said to me, his face so near mine I could smell his breath, but he pushed me and I fell back on the couch. I bounced up the way I always did while playing soccer and being knocked down by large men. I grabbed him around the trachea of his throat and slammed him against the wall, told him to never touch me again. Left red indents on his throat. This image of myself I have, fierce and uncompromising, completely over the bullshit of men, of their right to possess a woman, hold power over her personal space, feels like a feral magic that I wish I could bottle and drink from. This is not to say I am any less than I was in that moment, but somewhere along the way, battling illness and PTSD, I lost a bit of the confidence in my body. The woman in the mirror looks tired. She doesn't trust the construction of her body the way she once did. But in my mind, I am that woman walking away: changing her number and driving away from a man she loves on a logging road, spending a week with legs thrashing to escape her own addiction, a woman who had recently kissed death, body small and strong walking out the door of a party where whispers in the corner of her wild, crazy abandon followed her firm steps out of the door.

In a conversation with someone about these multiple selves I'm stacking here in these pages, they say, "Instead of where is she, the question could just as easily be, *when is she?*"

Taxidermied Love

IV.

Imagine kissing

you / on the streets / still throttle /

still bow / arrow / bruised

lips from the kill / still hunger /

still prowling / dusk until dawn.

Promises

Everything

only feel like home

My hand has been turning into a bear paw, tight from carpal tunnel and arthritis. My dominant hand curls in on itself, becomes wretched, becomes a claw. The other night I dreamt a bear, a tiger, and a wolf were stalking me through the woods. I climbed a tree to the top. They climbed the tree next to me. The tip of the tree was too thin. It started bending towards the ground. I thought, *Okay, when the tip touches the ground you must run the fastest you've ever ran.* And then I woke up. I think I am finally turning back into an animal; into the thing I should have been all along. I saw a hawk swooping between the winter trees and saw myself as a bear reach out and snatch it out of the air.

I want to write you blue letters from home. What I mean when I say that is: I want you to feel like the light after thick inches of snow pile up at dawn on the empty benches and pallet board chairs around the fire pit that's filled to the brim with ashes and then snow on top of ashes, pure glistening white to hide what is underneath. When I say blue letters what I mean is I want you to ache. Not a small ache. Not a twinge of something lost. Hollowed out. The kind that doesn't leave a *whole*. Like the space at the center of the cherry blossoms trunk that sits empty, that sits neglected, the place where the heart used to be and now all that's there is the burrowing, late February snow. When I say blue letters, imagine that you are the hyacinth my partner planted for me last Valentine's Day while I was at university, and then imagine that the next day, when you woke, you were buried past your nose in paper water, which is snow, which is what death probably feels like. And when the snow melts, you're dead, of course you're dead. You can't live without your darkness, which is me, which is what I want you to think of me, which is how you should remember me. As something you thought you had and lost but you never really had, and when you sleep at night you think I'm the moon watching over you, but the moon is just a cavern of dust, and I only write you blue letters when I can bury them here inside a longer letter that is really written to me and for me and not for you.

I'm just trying to whisper. *I am here.*

I dreamt my partner and I made love in a glass house. When people passed by, he tried to pull away, to scramble his clothes back into place. I locked my legs around him, prepared to expose myself to the world for a moment of feeling. When I woke, I couldn't be positive it was him I had dreamed of. The memory of the man felt like a compilation of every man I've ever offered my body to. Their hands will forever be on me. Here are the walls of my glass house. I want you to watch me yearn.

Up at Timberline Lodge on Mt. Hood it is Valentine's Day. *A* is out flying down the mountain at 44 mph, give or take. I am in the lodge near the fire reading, watching the snow fall, watching the embers burn low in the fire, watching the couples move in my orbit, capturing a crow fly by the window in the fog bank of snow, barely thinking. Our lives are separate, mine and *A*'s, mine and the people all around me. There is a couple across from me, the woman absentmindedly grasps the wool covered ankle of the man next to her on the couch. An older couple sits on a couch facing the snow looking down into books, into worlds, into themselves. A couple walks by looking for a spot to sit. "Feel free to sit here," I say, "I do not take up much space." Which of course, is a lie. "We're okay," the man in the plaid vest smiles, "Take up all the space you need." I think of how *A* will come in from the snow, bundled tightly, nose frost-bitten, sore and old. We will check into the last room available, a chalet with twin bunk beds, the epitome of romance. A person goes trundling by slowly in the snow. A bystander sits on a couch by the fire, wary.

In 21-degree weather and dropping, we made our way to the outdoor hot tub on Valentine's night. Snow piled up on the chairs and steps and walls around us. Mist rose off the hot water and confronted the frigid air creating a clashing cloud. The wind whipped through the night sky, exposing, then hiding pieces of the Mt. Hood, wild sky. The moon a half. Orion appeared to me. The tips of my short hair froze in the air, becoming crunchy and brittle. An older man joined us in the water. "Happy Valentine's," he said. "My honey is with me too, but she wasn't interested in the hot tub. I just turned 71 and tomorrow I get to ski for free. Apparently after you're 71 you get access to the mountain for free. Isn't that something?" After ten minutes in the hot water he wished us a good night and got out. He stood for a moment at the edge of the swimming pool. His body was slender but muscled. He tested the water with a foot. There, in the cold February moonlight reflecting off the quiet water, he drew his body up, mist rising around him, and dove into the glacial wet world.

At 5 a.m. our bodies pressed together in the bottom bunk of the twin-size bed found each other for the first time in months. The last time was early morning in a beachfront hotel. It is as if we must leave ourselves, our regular lives, to become others in the early morning. The snow piled so high that we couldn't see a hint of daylight out the long window. It is only in the dark, where I can't be seen, but felt, that I feel my body as sexy. Afterwards, we become ourselves again. We have re-inhabited our bodies. The spell is broken. Must we leave our home where our dogs lovingly sleep curved around our spines in our queen size bed to discover our own bodies? Even in order to climax I must step outside my body. I must imagine that the action is happening to someone else, to a body that is separate from my own, as if I am viewing it from above, from the crevasse the snow created between the window and the wall. I must watch my body from the outside-in.

Earl grey notes steep in the February sky, but they do not drip down on me, even when I want them to. The moss green is so vibrant today that I want to bathe in it. My body has been rejecting me the last few weeks. I can feel illness clawing up the sides of my throat, sometimes I choke on my own breath. It feels like a curse to write this down. I never want to admit when the waves are coming, as if penning it will make them real, solid, a tangible thing that I can't refuse. I am getting sick again, even though again is always now, there are just various levels. I'm wiped out by exhaustion. My intestines and stomach are distended again, swollen, violent. The headaches are increasing with rapid fire. I am on day 6 of one. Each night I wake up to pee I feel the throbbing in the back of my temple. *Hello, I am here.* My anxiety has been rearing; the nightmares have appeared with a sharp twang of denial. Focus doesn't come easy or at all. Sometimes I feel so weak and tired that my words begin to slur like a drunk man making his way through the dark streets, stumbling over his own two feet. The world seems so bright outside my back door. I imagine walking around the yard in moss and dewy grass, barefoot. I imagine building a fire and coming away smelling like smoke and camping and making love in the night. I think of raking up the leaves that fell in November, crowding the rose bushes on the front lawn. I imagine taking *A* into the fold of our forest-green painted room and fucking on the red and black checkered comforter. I imagine weeding the herb garden for the first time in months, hands coming away smelling like lemon thyme, rosemary, lavender, soil kisses. I curl into a thick blanket. I prop a book on the couch near where I rest my head. I disappear.

I went to get a tattoo on my right thigh by a friendly acquaintance from my hometown. We knew each other in the way that people whose lives circle each other know one another. I wore a white dress with the silhouette of black swallows on it to get my tattoo of a crow reading books on a river. I thought I would come home and write in a section about the proximity of hands to body parts that are rarely ever touched by anyone but me. I like the idea of everything being slightly erotic, though so few things actually are.

Reading *A Folded Clock: A Diary,* by Heidi Julavits has brought me to the realization that I am not the only one out there in the world trying to feel something, trying to catch a high, trying to live, trying to find out what it is like to die, trying to fall in love, catch the next wave, fight the next fight, read a book that devours you, see a piece of art that makes you weep, experience the world as if it were fresh, new, and broken open like the first bite of a sour apple from the crab apple tree. Like Heidi waiting for an elevator that never seems to come, I too am close to my breaking point.

Everything lately feels like a faraway dream. My brain fog has been so dense that I can't distinguish one thought from the next. I'll be trying to recall something that is at the cusp of my memory. The thought is almost there. I will feel a deep anxiety at the inability to grasp whatever it was that I am reaching for, then moments later I will become lost in the reverie of the trees swaying outside my window in the wind and want to take a nap. I lose my potency to feel desire, hunger, thirst. The only thing that is left in these times is fear and sleep. I gorge myself on a steady diet.

Every time the sky is bright blue, I think about kayaking. I think about kayaking a lot more than a woman of illness should. I imagine that maybe this is an activity I could do with illness, as long as the water is mostly still water. I just need a little pull, a little tug to help me move down stream. Kayaking seems to me to be a solitary un-solitary activity. I mention it at least ten times a year. I want to spend time with the water without having to actually get into the water. When I was young my mom called me a fish. My body already knew what it needed to do. I was part seal. I think about swimming all the time. Whenever the sky is blue. Every few weeks I look up swimming pools in my area, imagine paying a monthly fee to come and do laps. I am exhausted by the activity and eventually close the computer and lay back down.

My partner is a stocky, burly man. My roommate said when she thinks of him, she thinks of a bear. While looking at his pale freckled back this morning, I felt how fragile and vulnerable our bodies are. He hasn't started an accelerated aging process yet. His body isn't trying to destroy itself from the inside out, slowly, systemically. I wondered, what will be the first to begin shutting down on him. His back? This powerful spine and torso. I imagine it hunched, knots down his spine, back surgeries where he would be laid out for months. *No*, I think, *it will probably be his knees that go first, buckled under him*. His bear body a lumbering strength that will eventually bring him to the ground.

I don't remember anything about when I died from my ectopic pregnancy. I remember, before going under anesthesia, the cerulean eyes of the technician who put me under. I've wondered if he was an angel. I am wondering it now. Whenever I read about someone's death experience, what they saw, a tight fist forms in my abdomen. My heart stopped twice, but I don't remember anything. There must have been something though, because when I came out, I told my mom I thought that my grandma told them to let me go, that it wasn't my time yet. Was this something I experienced or something I wanted to believe? It is something I still want to believe. When I try to reach for that blank space, I find nothing there. It is a void. It is empty. No wonder my PTSD is so violent whenever my heart flutters remotely the way it did on the day it stopped. I am terrified that there is nothing after. I am envious of those with religion to guide them. I am determined to become a ghost and wander forever. An eternal between place is better than no place at all. I want to believe that when I die there will be someone on the other side waiting for me. My grandmother in her white walking sneakers will reach through the veil, walk me to a porch in the sunrise, and rub the sleep from my hands and feet.

I need to get to the ocean. When was the last time my toes kissed sand? I am in love with a world that doesn't always love me back, a body that is relentless and unforgiving in its pursuit of illness, a mind filled with all the men I've loved and the women who've loved me and the things I can't begin to let go of.

If I knew how to ask for love would you take my hand?

My roommate tossed her phone down on my bed. "Why do I want everything that isn't mine or that I can't afford. When will this desire to have and be everything end?"

Talking about a book my sister was reading in which the protagonist murdered her husband after years of being beaten by her husband we all nodded in agreement that the woman had done the right thing. My mom said, "I almost hired a hit man once." She looked across the table at me. I wondered if she meant hired one to take out my biological father, a man who beat her. This isn't my story though it is a part of my story. She once called the cops on him. This was the early 90's. When they arrived, he told the cops she had fallen down the stairs and hit her face on my crib. They left. "How did you find the hitman?" I asked. "I didn't," she said, "it was someone I already knew who knew what was happening. He offered. It would have cost me a 6-pack of beer." I sat there thinking about men who want to suffocate the light out of you and about the women, the ones here at this table, who didn't let them.

I woke up soaked in sweat from a fever dream. I changed my pajamas in the dark. When I awoke in the morning, I began bleeding at first light. This is what it is like to be a woman. The world is never done reminding you that your body should make something. Even when your body refuses.

"Shortly after you almost died from your ectopic rupture, I was having really bad pains in my pelvis," my sister said. "We had been trying to get pregnant for a while, and I had never felt pains like that before. I went into the ER, not knowing what else to do. The doctor told me it was just my ovaries, that the pain was me ovulating. She said it to me like I was so stupid, and she couldn't believe I had come in and wasted her time."

In *Motherhood*, by Sheila Heti, she seeks out what it is like to be any and every woman. The motherless, the childless, the child-bearing, the artist coupled, the artist alone on a cliffside creating art and questioning everything and questioning nothing. It is much the way that I am using this manuscript to explore the options of having options, of going back in time to other loves, of remembering myself as not sick, a dream of creating in myself an immoral person, a person whose sexual being surpasses that of what she is, what I actually am. In it I can be the type of person who thinks about having an affair, who is having an affair, who has sex with other people in her dreams, who becomes a mountain of a woman. Then, when I am ready, I can close the laptop and walk away. I can set the dream person aside. When I am ready to be someone other, I can return to the pen, to the computer, to the idea that I have not made my choices already.

I wrote to my mentor, "So, what do I even know about the world? Nothing."

The winter is hard and unruly, and I need to go out into the world. I need to watch the ants in their march, and the birds in their flight, and the grass make waves, and the trees whistle. I need to move my body around on the earth. I need to remember what it can do so when I return home, I have something to say. So many times, I think that I want to garden, or go swimming, or take a pottery class, a painting class, learn how to refinish furniture properly. I want to be a writer who has something more to say than that illness is crawling around inside my body like a slippery snake and I sit back and let it.

I dreamt that I was on a road trip with my partner. It was the middle of the night and we stopped at a gas station. I tried to fuck him there in the parking lot, but he refused me. Then, I dreamt that I was staying at a hotel with my ex. He never refused me, but when I woke inside the dream he was gone. I found him sleeping out in the hallway, a copy of my book held tightly in his hand. I urgently went back to my hotel room to write this all down. Later, in a dream version of Astoria, I wandered the town in my bare feet. The ground was thick with water and moss, the trees thrashed above me. I couldn't find my ex-lover. He disappeared again. On the ground were hundreds of baby crocodiles trying to bite my toes. When I woke up in the morning, I couldn't say with one-hundred percent certainty who it was I tried to fuck in the car at the gas station and who I'd fucked in the hotel room.

When I was no more than a toddler, I'd drape my body over couch ends, press my pelvis to the hard bar hidden under the cushioned arm. I'd leave the couch feeling exhausted and exhilarated. It reminded me of running. I called it my exercises. In elementary school, while reading our giant textbooks in class aloud, I would press the spine of the book to my pelvis. For my first 4 years of sex, it was almost always in the woods or in my car or in my or my boyfriend's bedroom. There has almost always been an element of thievery to getting off. The first year with my partner involved a lot of front-seat fucking. Once, we did it on the back counter at a pizza joint where he worked. He told me, "This is where we make the pizzas." As if the gleaming clean blades of the pizza cutters didn't tell me all I need to know. Now that I can do it in the comfort of my own home, I almost never want to, and when I do I often imagine that someone is looking through the window or that there is someone in the next room getting off to the sound of me getting off. I have a deep desire to be known, to be seen.

Nobody talks about female masturbation or desire, least of all the males. And even the females, when they do, it's in hushed tones and filled with remorseful giggles. It's 2019 women, wake up and smell your own hunger. I write this as I continue to have zero communication with my partner of almost eight years about my body as liquid Viagra. But, then again, nobody talks about problems of the vagina either. I know plenty of women with a tilted uterus. They say it like a curse. It is only ever mentioned once. 1 in 5 women have my condition, vulvar vestibulitis, but I'm the only one I've ever heard utter its name outside of the one female doctor who, after years of painful intercourse, gave it a name. It sounds like a plague of the heart. The other day my 29-year-old partner referred to the vagina as a jinny. "Don't say it like that. What are you, four?" I said.

Most of the time when I am feeling horny around bedtime, I force myself to go to sleep without getting myself off while my partner plays video games in the living room. I don't do this out of some weird sort of penance or aversion to the touch of my own skin. I do it because if I go to bed with a throbbing between my lips, I'll dream about having sex with someone. When I do give in to my desires, I always regret it. No matter how tired I was before I started, I can never sleep afterwards and that night my dreams will be nightmares or empty.

Visiting my hometown of Astoria is like entering into a dream from which I never actually left. We pull in after dark. The fog is beginning to creep up from the river and slide its way up the hills. Everywhere I look I see the ghost of a boy I loved walking the streets, past the cemetery, walking the same circles he grew up on, a shadow of a shadow of a former self. Wherever I look, it's like I'm seeing two splices of film draped over top each other.

The first night home for a four-day trip I stay at my partner's parents' house with the dogs while he stays at his best friend's. The dogs keep me up all night, circling, fearing that they are missing out on some excitement in the wild backyard of his parents' house. Deer to bark at, cats to smell in the distance. I wake up at 2 a.m. and look at the glare of my phone. I've missed a call from him, but when I call back it goes straight to voicemail. My youngest dog lays near my face all night and every hour or so cry-whimpers into it, wondering where his dad is. When I finally wake up to the daylight I step outside with my tea and discover daffodils and crocuses blooming in the backyard.

While driving after brunch with an old friend who was only two months clean from heroin, we were talking about other people who weren't clean or had overdosed recently. Going up over the hill we passed someone the boys used to know. Our friend said, "Should we pick him up? Should we just go around picking up familiar strangers. People we used to know."

I dreamt that I couldn't leave my house. I was stuck there for fifteen days, but they were repeat days, like I was stuck in a movie. On the fifteenth day I found the necklace that I needed in order to leave. While I was out at the mall shopping, I clutched the necklace in a fist around my throat, terrified that I would lose my ability to leave my house again. I stepped into a stairwell and the top stair collapsed beneath my feet.

I went sea-glass hunting with my best friend on the Washington side of the Megler bridge. We could see our hometown stretched out before us while the waves of the mouth of the Columbia River thrashed against the sand. We went at low-tide and fell into a vacuum of time. For two hours we wandered in mostly opposite directions. I would look up to see her silhouette in the distance, crouched over rocks, sifting. I came across a bone and a crow, and the wind rustled briskly through my thin spring jacket.

At lunch, talking about the tantalizing lazy days of summer that were only months away, I exclaimed how I would miss watching my niece and nephew this summer, but how I am also grateful to have my summer days back. I joke that whatever god is up there knew that I shouldn't actually have children when he made me. I don't have the patience for children. They couldn't have taken this right away from a better candidate. I love my alone time too much. Hours after that, upon returning to *A*'s parent's house, I walked into the living room to see him holding his two-year-old nephew, smiling and chattering happily with him. He would make a good dad, I thought. At dinner that night with his family, as we looked over at his nephew's smiling face, his mom said, "If you guys have a kid, he'd look just like that, only he'd be calmer." Despite having told her previously that I can't have children, instead of telling her again I said, "I don't know about that. I was a terror when I was a child. They called me a monster. I bit my sister. I colored on everything: the walls, the heater vents while they were turned on so that the crayons melted into them, even on a dress once while my sister was wearing it."

98

I woke to go to the bathroom. I turned to shut the door so the dogs wouldn't escape and wake up the rest of *A*'s family. Out the window, merely two feet from where I had been resting my head, stood two deer. One stared into the room at me while the other kept grazing in the early light of dawn.

I dreamt I was taking a painting class. There were no walls in the room and the wind blew my hair all around me. I painted in a fever of color; my body splattered in the paint. When we returned the next day one of my peers had written a story in paint overtop my art, and the picture I was painting could no longer be seen.

While walking out of the woods and down a path with friends, I leaned on *A* heavily, pestering him to carry me, not thinking that he would. Suddenly, he swooped me up in both arms, the sun peering down between branches, and I laughed joyously, feeling like an empress being carried on a bed made of silk. Later, at the teahouse, while I chose which pot of tea would suit the afternoon, he rubbed my shoulders lightly, something he usually does not do. Walking back from a talent show his nieces performed in, the chill of the coastal evening settling into my skin, I pushed him and raced on ahead. He caught up and pretended that he was going to bump me into the street. His sea blue eyes twinkled, and I thought, *how lucky I am to have this man with a jovial and light heart.*

I dreamt I was at my high school in Wyoming surrounded by all my peers, except for my first boyfriend and oldest friend who passed away at 27 from cancer. We were all graduating, except for Jeremy, and I wept openly that he would never get to graduate with us, even though in the waking world he had graduated, and those of us still left are nearing 30. In the dream I moved outside, where I found my oldest friend of 17 years sitting on a bench waiting for his girlfriend to come get him. It seemed that every line of color was fluorescent. I sat down next to him, weary, I rested my head on his shoulder. His body began a slow turn towards me, and he kissed me tentatively. Then he kissed me like we were drowning. I woke up to the sound of a light kiss near my ear. I tried to fall back into the dream, but the dogs were awake, the room was cold and morning light crept over my head through the window, and that dream was a place I was never meant to go. The dream colored my day, a questioning mountainside view. I thought about calling my friend. I imagined visiting with him one day and asking if he'd ever thought about *us* in all the years that have passed. Why do I constantly feel as if I've misplaced things I've never had?

I spend more time than I'd like to admit imagining what would happen if *A* left me or if I left him or if he died.

We are all wandering around, filled with life, wondering who we could have or might end up being. The only thing standing between us and who we think we are, who we think we might be, if given the chance, is a wall that needs torn down, a subway train, an unfinished canoe, a book that hasn't been written, an apartment that has never been left.

After finishing *Sylvia*, by Leonard Michaels, I had a dream that the man I loved, who was a version of Sylvia, called me. I hid in a tiny closet sized bathroom to take his call. He said, "I still feel we are two pieces of a puzzle. I still love you. Don't you love me?" My dream self said, "I don't know."

It would be a lie to say I didn't feel a confusing and strange nostalgia masquerading as desire. It is an exquisite and ruinous experience, love like I once had, so violent in its hunger, that any other version of love feels comfortable and boring, almost maddening. But that wasn't healthy love. You shouldn't hate, in equal parts, the one you love.

Yesterday, my mom said to my brother about her mentally abusive husband that she divorced after 3 months, "I couldn't go or do anything without him. I had to ask permission to go get groceries. And unlike Shilo's dad, who beat me, the mental abuse was far worse. But over time, I got stronger. It built up, until I left. That doesn't happen for most people." My brother took a drag off his cigarette. "I wish you'd told a different story," he said. "There is no other story," I said, "This is her story. It is the only one she has to tell."

I silently judge those close to me who insist on verbally rehashing out details of their broken hearts. Don't they know these are the things best kept close to the lining of the body? *Poor child*, I think, as I come to the page to place the pieces of my own broken heart. The burden is too heavy to carry it on my own after all this time. Driving home from work the Rascal Flatts song "What Hurts the Most", came on the radio while a spring rain fell upon the world. It was the song that was playing the night I gave away my virginity to my first love. That was over thirteen years ago. I found myself crying on the way home. When another driver almost ran me out of my lane and into another car I blasted on my horn. *Can't you see I'm trying to mourn here*!

I pulled over on the hill to scribble down a note: I want to be done searching the landscapes looking for lost loves.

my heart broke
for love

Taxidermied Love

V.

Lovers—ghosts—tuck my
lust into your pocket, a
kerchief of secrets.
Quiet thrum of jackalope
fearsome horned crush of desire.

The thunder is rumbling outside my window and the moss on the branches of the gum tree makes me think about being haunted and I like it. I want to be haunted by the ghost of lost and unknown loves until the day I die and when I die, I wouldn't be mad if more than one man was seen wearing all black, standing back from my grave under the shade of an old oak tree, crying silent tears into the rain.

I want to be done pretending that I'm not scouring the landscape in pursuit of love.

If I am anything, I am vast. This is just a pretentious way to say that I want many things all at one time and my hunger devours me, making me question my comfortable life at every turn.

I find myself attracted to a visual artist despite my impulse to not be attracted to her. Currently, she is sitting across the room from me, alternating between journaling and staring out the window into the rainy forest scene. We are listening to her playlist, and in a different world, I could imagine this as our meet-cute, but this is the world of reality and I am not in a dream.

Here I am, dreaming into people again.

Looking at her black underwear, visible through her stretched yoga pants as she hunches over her work, I felt a throbbing, like an opening in my body as I allow myself to be attracted to anyone my body wants to be attracted to.

It appears my body is not yet done with desire.

I return to the cabin where two women who arrived together discuss art quietly at the table and the woman who is staying in the tent is lying face down on the patio absorbing the world. I sit by the window writing and watch as she lifts herself, makes her way bare footed down to the creek where she returns moments later holding a flower. One of the women behind me says, "I woke up thinking about green."

On the morning of an artist retreat, I am cradling Mary Oliver with the morning chill creeping through the wood walls. I picture the other women, delicate in sleep, bodies curved. A half-moon. The one with the spiral red hair up in the loft of the cabin, scrawling poetry while her companion sleeps. The companion, limbs long and towering, hair buzzed down, twisted into fresh sheets: an extravagant snail shell tucked in. The dark-haired girl in the tent nearby, flat on her stomach, slender legs unclothed, touched by a thin mist, dreaming about the river crackling by. And me, my tea in hand, romanticizing watching a robin hop-hop along the green grass, staring up into the dense trees, imagining what the bear dreams about when she sleeps.

So many things in life happen slowly, on extended time. Falling out of love, for instance, takes about ten years, by my calculations. Realizing you've made decisions over those last ten years based on the misinformation given to you by your twenty-year old broken-hearted self, and the world is a slow burn, a gradual move to acknowledgement. Some things, instead, are fast. The force violent, even, in the way you are forever changed, as if you have been running around in a field and are trapped and struck down in an electric storm.

A came home from work. My body had been throbbing all day. He wanted to leave to run an errand. I pressed my body to his. He took me back to our bedroom. We fucked and I gripped the metal bedframe the way I imagined doing since we added the bed frame six months ago. Afterwards, laying on my stomach, naked in the afternoon light and inhabiting my body in a way I never do, he kissed the skin of my butt cheek lightly and I thought, *I could live like this forever.*

I dreamt a man I didn't know leaned over and whispered in my ear. My stomach fluttered and I followed him down a long hallway.

I dreamt that I was talking to *A*. We were at a bus stop that stretched wide in both directions. I turned around and when I turned back, he was instead my first love. It started to rain on us. "I won't kiss you," he said, "but I still think about you every time it rains."

It seems that all I have left is control.

During a yoga meditation class, we were told to breathe into the center of our body, to follow the energy to the heart of our body. The teacher said, "Listen to the heart of your body for a wish." I breathed in deeply, eyes closed loosely, the energy building in the center of my belly.

I can't do it all over again: be a child making mud-pies in the side yard, run naked in the woods for the first time, lay on the rug at my mom's feet while she reads us children's books, fall in love for the first time, ride around in my sister's first car blasting early 2000's hits. This feeling overtakes me at random moments; I want to drop to my knees and openly weep in my backyard, in the street, in the grass full of strangers swaying to music at a concert. I want to cry for the child, teenager, young woman I'll never again be.

Mary Oliver asks where are the people who wake in the night and sing. I want to do just that. Her lines alone make my body ache, but instead I curl into bed and wake up on and off throughout the night overcome with something I can't name, wondering if everyone else in the world allows themselves to feel more alive than me.

When I'm driving down a dark road looking out at the silhouetted tree line, which somehow looks the same no matter where I am, I imagine I could have a million other lives, be a different person, know what it is like to eclipse my own desire.

The sunflowers in the August Oregon heat are drooping their heads toward the ground and I gather crow feathers wherever they fall.

I fell in love in December, a couple days after my sixteenth birthday. The boy I fell in love with was complicated. He had already been in and out of juvenile detention and rehab many times. He was a child, but his light was very dark. He was an addict and when he was using, he was abusive. He had many relations with other girls, and over the years I was with him, I would find myself in and out of a toxic, mentally and sexually abusive relationship that was also sometimes a loving and supportive relationship. I was a child, but I began having adult trauma, adult depression and anxiety. I knew about things I shouldn't. During that time period I would become many things.

"I don't have much interest in men lately," I told my mom over tea.

It's difficult to write nonfiction as a practice. It's nearly impossible to write it when you aren't living honestly to begin with. Authenticity is the key to life, and life is the key to reach the words and the words are a key to...

What are words a key to?

If I knew my own heart, I wouldn't find it so god damn fleeting. I wouldn't be filled with a constant dread that I'm settling in one or more capacity. Some days I think nothing at all. Today, the edges of the gum tree leaves are turning red. I haven't been fucked in three months, but whenever the offer is made, I turn away from it. I'm a maudlin twenty-nine-year-old woman and my heart is in a box.

The first friend I tried to tell that I was bisexual said, "I think you're confusing sexuality with your desire." I shook my head, "No," I said, "When I watch porn, I often look at the women." I didn't tell her that sometimes I look up videos with only women. "That's because you're interested in the act of sex, not just the women," she said, with authority.

There once was a time where I tracked time by its alignment between another body and mine. If one body is the sun and one is the moon what are the hours of the day where the two will meet? I wasn't tracking time so much as tracking the void where you weren't. There was no time in waiting for your call, only a series of things I did to will away the hours. But something happens, when your time becomes only for another: there is a trick of the light, the world flattens on its axis. It doesn't spin anymore. There became only where I was and where you weren't.

Unfortunately, that means time has shifted altogether, for the rest of my time before my bones return to soil, maybe not even then. It's not the spaces. Distance, it turns out, is not the thing that keeps us apart. It's me. I needed a timeline that moved forward, that didn't spin on your axis. I need fields to walk through, not a labyrinth.

I turn thirty and the world doesn't stop. I pass the place from which I died, another rotation on my moon. I haven't written about the heart in eight months. I fell down a well of imagination during the summer, imagined that, if given the chance I could fall in love. I incubated the love for my partner, weighed it against passion, curled into its comfort.

I told my mom a few weeks prior that I felt I was finally falling out of love with my first love after almost ten years apart, but each night the chill of frost approaches, the time of year is coming when I met him, when I first fell in love, and then years later the same time of year when I nearly died from a ruptured ectopic pregnancy I got from going back to him, going back on a promise to myself, and each night, like clockwork, I dream of him. The old quotes come to me. I feel a wounded animal, shot in the ankle and left in the cold, white snow to die. I feel the crisp break of my favorite turquoise crayon snapped in half. *I'll never be out of this*, I think. I watch the early winter chill blow through the October trees and think, *I'll never want to.*

I dreamt that I was pregnant. A girl. I dreamt that my ex, this time around a decent man, and yes, still in love with me, was there, but he wasn't the father. I wanted him to be the father, but he wasn't. When I told him this, that it was a man I couldn't remember, a young man, one I had slept with and was blacked out of my memory, a thing I did in heartbreak, the man I still loved whose baby I did not carry took my hand and kissed it softly.

It isn't until I see a person who, days prior, I hadn't loved, leaning against a dorm bed in sweatpants, New Hampshire summer sunlight streaming on their face, that I realize I can fall in love with others. That I am something I never thought I'd be again. And when I return home, I dream of them in that dorm room. Each dream I am undressed.

I write you a letter and tell you that I dreamt of you, that I dreamt I buried myself in snow and became a tree. I'm not a tree, but I'd be one if you asked me to be.

Six months later, in the depths of New Hampshire winter, I try to look the other way, avert my eyes, make the choice not to blow up my life. But when you read aloud, each pause weighted, your voice a quiet rumble in my soul, I try not to cry. I try not to imagine what it'd be like to have you read me poetry every night in bed. A shiver travels down my spine and I am undone.

Imagine me dipping my fingers into the cool wisped chestnut of your hair. Imagine me fondling the peach frond of your earlobe, my chin against the bristle of the hay fever growing on your chin. Imagine us stark, crisply entwined, the looming New Hampshire winter around us. Us, a snuck kiss, me in the passenger seat, you, a silhouette shining through the winter night, a halo of snow falling around. Us, in a vacuum, our voices disappearing into midnight. Imagine me returning to the west coast, us in separate worlds, snuggled around our dogs. Imagine the letters unanswered, the guilt nagging me in my secure life, my passions untold. Imagine me on your doorstep, knocking, knocking, knocking. No one answers and I find blue eyes looking out at me through every home.

I say, in a room filled with other people, "I just need to stop talking." And you say, "No, never stop talking." And I can't tell, do you mean: You're my friend and I think you're funny and I like to hear what you have to say. Or, do you mean, *Please, don't ever go away.*

I don't even need to do it, pull the trigger. I've already lived it, built the entire fantasy of us into my mind. But that doesn't mean I won't think about it, that doesn't mean I won't replay a kiss that never happened like the greatest hits reel.

"Write me letters," I say, "but I won't hold it against you if you don't." You say, "I've already written it and will put in the mail tomorrow." And I try not to stand out in the January rain waiting for the mailman to come.

I woke gasping under the weighted, plaid comforter on my bed. In my dream I had been to the hospital. "I heard my mom had a heart attack. I need you to tell me, is she in a coma, or is she dead?" I asked the woman at the desk. She searched my mother's name on the computer screen. "It appears she has left permanently. She is dead." I bent down, gripping the counter with pressed-white fingers, crying so deeply that when I catapulted awake, my breath was ragged and there were tears in the corners of my eyes. All morning I waited for a message from my mom. I didn't want to tell her what I had dreamed. Her mom died at 54 from a heart attack. I am not a prophet. I only know what my ghosts have seen.

Talking to my partner about some of his co-workers who have been on-again-off-again for years I ask, "What would you do if we ever broke up? Would you Tinder?" I don't wait for his answer, "I can't imagine Tindering, can't imagine meeting people in such an impersonal way. That sounds terrifying." He laughs but never says.

I meet my younger sister from my biological father whom I haven't seen since I was 12 and she was 7 or 8. I am now thirty. I have another, older sister who I've never met, she has a different mom than both of us. At the end of the night my little sister tells me that, because of our older sister being a lesbian she hasn't been accepted by the older generations on my biological father's side. "I wouldn't care," I say. "My uncle is gay and married and I am bisexual." It is the first time I say it out loud, without telling someone in a roundabout way. My boyfriend, a bit drunk, says, "You don't know that for sure." And I think I could lay him out right there, all two hundred something pounds of him. After they leave, I say, "Don't you dare ever undermine my sexual identity like that again." He clams up. "For your information, I do know. I've known now for five fucking years, it just so happens I've been with you the whole time, but guess what: the book I've been writing about desire is also about me being attracted to other genders, dreaming about sex with them, I have kissed a woman before and liked it, and half the time when I watch porn there are no men in it." He tries to take ownership of this part of me, turn it into something to use for his pleasure by laughing and suggesting we watch lesbian porn together. I turn from him. "I will never do that for you." I walk away.

I was thinking about lost boys in small towns. I was thinking about that time a drunken boy who I made out with once, and who groped my boobs so roughly that he left dark purple bruises that lasted for weeks before they turned an ugly yellow, a boy who called me drunk late one night from outside my parent's home, and when I told him to leave, flipped a U-turn in his giant diesel truck up over my neighbor's yard. In the morning I discovered tire marks through their grass. Later in the day I learned of a wreck that occurred on the backroads. A blue diesel truck had a head-on collision with a power pole. Luckily, he hadn't been wearing his seat belt, and his loose drunk body flew through his open window, landing with no broken bones before running drunken, into the night.

I'm not sure what this has to do with desire, but all bad stories can become good stories if you line up the words right.

Sometimes I think I have a perfectly okay life. Other days I think, *Is this really all that there is?*

When I was a young girl a relative once said, "Good lord, look at the length of that child's lashes. She is going to be a heartbreaker." I heard it as I went running by, my yellow hair whipping out behind me. There always comes a point, in every relationship I've ever been in, where I know I will leave the man I love.

One morning, recently, I woke crying. I cried in the shower. I cried standing in the door, the chill of early winter wind swaying the trees while my dogs ran around chasing invisible squirrels, maybe the ghost of the squirrel paralyzed from a fall and murdered by my neighbor. I cried on and off all day until my partner came home, thinking that when he arrived it was going to be the end of us, suddenly, after eight years, we were going to have to decide how to share the dogs, and I was going to have to move back in with my parents who are now in their fifties and I am no longer a child. We did not break up. I did not move home. But, I discovered, I'm thirty years old and I've never been responsible for my entire self. I've never lived alone, and have been a relatively kept woman, for all my empowered ideas.

It is hard, being a bird without wings.

When I tell *A* I want to go into the woods to track down a waterfall on the Washington side of the gorge, he insists I not go into the woods alone. He is worried about me getting lost or possibly running into a cougar. I am not as worried about these things. When I think about going into the woods alone, I am worried about men that might also be in the woods alone.

I can only write stories where people don't talk to each other and everything has already happened.

My roommate is being pressured by her co-workers to ask out a guy who works at the bar near their workplace. When she tells them no, she says, "I like the slow-burn."

Poem 6

Forget
Erase
Try

Taxidermied Love

VI.

I searched the socials
for your likeness, found only pale
impersonators
talons with no beak, birds with
no fight, empty nests, blight.

I dreamt I went on a holy pilgrimage up flights and flights of stairs. By the time I reached the top I was weeping, ready to admit that I want a different life than the one I have. When I left the pilgrimage, I found my partner and picked a fight so that I could leave him. Later in the dream, I sought out the lover my dream-self wanted, and we set out across the desert together. They said they wanted to walk me home. When the ground crumbled beneath our feet, we shared our first kiss in the belly of a cave.

Writing these words often feels like watching a car wreck in slow motion.

I heard my roommate whisper to my dog, "I miss you when you're right in front of me."

I receive a letter from someone in my program asking what I see when I look at the moon. I read the letter twice and for hours after I hear a quote from the poet, Paige Ackerson-Kiely, repeated in my head except the word *book* has been replaced with the word *letter*. "I read your *letter* and I could die anywhere." Ever since receiving this letter the moon seems to be appearing everywhere. I look up at my bookcase to see the Moon in various titles. In *The Crying Book* Heather Christle writes, "A person who 'cries for the moon' wants too much—wants, in fact, more wanting—weeps into the lack. You can't make a wish upon the moon."

I got a tattoo of a window, then I read *The Taiga Syndrome*, by Cristina Rivera Garza, which is filled with windows and the character spends a great deal of time staring out them, staring into them, imagining what is on the otherside of them, imagining other people looking at her on the inside.I wake up one morning and, after smoking a joint in bed, get up to write a melancholy and dreamy work of connected flash fiction pieces about people staring out windows. A friend sends me a picture of the view out of her school window in Boston overlooking a graveyard. "I wish I was sitting next to you looking out the window at ghosts," I wrote back.

"I've never been in unrequited love," I tell my roommate. "Everyone I've ever loved has loved me back." Nowadays who I see in the mirror doesn't match my previous fire. I used to smolder under my skin. It used to rise to the top and reach out to everyone around it. I never was a great beauty, but my fever burned so bright. What has happened? I could fall drop down in love with someone and I don't think they'd even see me. The one under this tired skin.

Never mind that every day, a man comes home to me who loves me in quiet, tender, and secret ways that I know nothing about.

If gravitational forces could propel a person, my feet would be planted on the Atlantic shore. I project myself miles and miles from where I am. What is the use of nerve endings if I never put them to use? And who says it's no good, that I can't start where you begin?

I post the ending of a poem from TC Tolbert's *Gephyromania* online, and the friend who told me that this book is their bible wrote in response, "That poem! That ending! Ugh. 'How do you even love wholly & always?' Who even knows."

I respond: "loving wholly & always is best done from afar. Or so says my experience of love, which is limited at best, riddled with holes at worst." But what I want to say is, *Let me show you how.* But I don't say that and what I do say elicits no response.

We've officially entered dream season. Winter is nearing, we've already had first frost in mid-October, earlier than usual for the Willamette Valley. It is this time of year that my dreams become treacherous, treasonous. In their wake I become susceptible to the moods and actions that I experience in them. I know it is directly related to my young self's numerous traumas which were plentiful in the long, hollow months of December.

I'm trying not to explode my life. I'm trying to be present. I'm trying to remember that the person I come home to is the kind of man who gets teary eyed at Stars Wars when, for a moment, he thinks Chewbacca has died, or, again, at *The Dark Knight Rises*, when he thinks that Alfred the butler has died, or, while attending an intervention for a friend who has relapsed with heroin. I am trying to think of our lives with our dogs and the way he lifts our old dog up onto the bed every night and we all cry out, "Flying potato!" I am trying not to think of the New Hampshire summer heat, the blue heron that flew under my body while sitting on the edge of a covered bridge in Henniker reading poetry in the early hours of the morning. I'm trying not to think about the blue of New Hampshire winter, of walking by the river frozen in ice, of a life where I might walk to the college in this small town, teach classes on literature and writing, return down the river path to a small home where I drink tea by a window and read all through the night. I snuggle my dogs close to my body now and wait for him to come home. A playlist I built on my phone titled "New Hampshire Blue, New Hampshire You" plays softly in the background.

A coworker and I were talking about struggling in our long-term relationships. Speculating on how one is supposed to know when it is worth the time you're putting into it or when it is time to let it go. "I'm trying not to stay for the sake of staying, because staying is easier than leaving, but it is hard to know where the line is," she says. A customer comes to the counter and we help them. As they are walking away, I say, "Unfortunately, I think it's one of those things where you won't know until you know. You won't know with certainty until after you pull the trigger."

I'm terrified this book will get picked up and my life will implode.

I'm terrified this book will get picked up and my life won't implode.

We live in a culture that turns our noses down at struggle. Attaching your life to another person's is a struggle. There is no picture-perfect recipe to an always good relationship. There are things missing, things lost, things unknown out in the world and competing with your own desire, with your own fantasies of the other possible lives you may live is a good way to be sure the ship you're on will sink. But, but it is natural to question our choices. If you are not questioning what you're doing, are you even thinking?

Talking to a poet who also has Hashimotos and other chronic conditions she said, "Every doctor I've ever been to has tried to put me on anxiety meds when I told them I couldn't breathe. Finally, I went to see a throat and nose specialist, and it turns out that my breathing passages have been collapsing." Horrified, I told her that yes, every doctor I've known, even my naturopath wants to put me on anxiety meds as well, "But I don't want to quiet the sound of my body. I want to hear what it has to tell me." Nodding, she said, "Yes, they want to silence us. They just want us to shut up, so they won't have to hear what we are saying."

At winter residency I lay sick in bed from a terrible bout of acid reflux and a panic attack. After shuffling like an invalid down to the help desk to get some almond milk, I tried to quiet my body. A friend I was rooming with came in and talked to me until 3 am about love, about open relationships and the different ways that love manifests in the body. After a few hours my body finally stopped spasming in after-shock waves of muscle convulsions. Even the thought of love can be a balm for my suffering.

On a drive home from a movie *A* was a bit drunk. We were talking about how he needs to go in for a check-up because he hasn't been to a doctor in eight years and we both recently turned 30. "What am I supposed to do if something happens to you 'cause you're not monitoring your blood pressure that was already high at 22?" He laughed, "You're always saying you're going to leave me, so you'll be fine." Under the stoplight I turn to him, my hands gripping the wheel. "I'm sorry, but I just don't know what I want ever." But he was already on to the next subject as the light turned green.

I told a coworker that I had been in love with my first love for years, but, finally, over the last year, felt like I had fallen out of love with him. "I don't think I'm still in love with my first love," she said, "but I still dream of him. He haunts me." That night there was a jumbled dream; in it there was one clear moment. My first love was there. He turned and his eyes crinkled tight in the corners while he full-body laughed.

In, *The Taiga Syndrome*, Cristina Rivera Garza writes: "I was facing someone—I told myself several times, just to remember what was so obvious that it could become transparent and pass unperceived—who had managed to transform the world, or at least what was around her, into a world of her desires. A trembling image, something that gleams. What is between imagining a forest and living in a forest? What brings together the writing of a forest with the lived experience of a forest?"

I dreamt I walked up the hill at Shivley Park in my hometown and wept as I watched them chop down a tree where I used to meet you. I followed a trail from the park that lead me to a garage where I found you. You were so happy to see me. Your mom and sister watched on in joy as I ran to you. You took my face in your hands. Later, I was in an old Victorian house overlooking the Columbia River and my garden was filled with tall dune grass. I called to ask when you would be joining me. *I can't return with you to the sea.* I shut myself in a small closet. No, no, no, I said, tapping the back of my head on the wall.

I wonder how long it would take me to feel disquieted and ungratified in whatever imagined new life I could build for myself.

But then I wonder if love ever really goes away or if it just changes shape. I transform the love I have for you into something more productive than just dreams. It becomes a letter on a page, a song in my head upon waking up, everything, everything, everything.

I watch the black and white foreign film, *Elisa & Marcela*, when no one is home. I watch it in pieces. In one scene the women make love with the pressure of octopus tentacles draped over their breasts. In another, one woman comes home to find the other naked on the bed, seaweed twined around the limbs over her body. In another, one pours milk on the other's body while she tenderly kisses her.

Driving a friend just out of rehab back to the coast, he told us about a girl he's in love with and how she'd never been loved properly before. He said, "I told her love isn't ownership and that I just want her to be happy, that there are all kinds of love." To lighten the mood, I turned to *A* and said, "You don't know any of the types." We all laughed, then he said, "No, you don't know how to love." We laughed again. "That's probably true," I said. "SUCCUBUS!" He shouted.

On the series remake of *Four Weddings and a Funeral* one of the characters inquires about their new relationship. "There is that spark though, right?" Their friend asks. Later at work, a coworker tells me about seeing a guy who she sometimes dated back in high school. "Do you think it is just for funsies? Or do you have the spark?" I asked. She shrugged and giggled, "I don't know," she said while filling the popcorn kernel bin. The sounds of hundreds of small beads folding over each other vibrated around us. I leaned in conspiratorially, "If you did, you'd know."

When I am horribly sick to my stomach, laid up from a migraine, down in the depths of a panic attack and spinning from nausea, there is nothing I want more (besides relief) than to be at my home near my dogs and *A*.

As I lay in bed on the tail end of an hours long panic attack and stomach related illness flair, I keep nodding out only to be jolted awake by the sensation that I can't breathe. It wasn't until I rested my hand on the top of A's snoring head, his hair in my fingers, that I fell asleep.

After alternating between migraines and headaches for two weeks I make my first ever appointment with a massage therapist. Immediately upon seeing me she knows what I've been suffering. We talk nearly the whole appointment as she rubs down my body. We discuss illness, trauma, meditation, gratitude, abuse. Halfway through, while she is working on the top of one thigh, I still haven't relaxed. "I've been trying this whole time to be less tense, and it is just not working. I feel so rigid, but I am, in general, very uncomfortable being touched." She says something about our parent's generation not being much for physical affection and how that has messed us up because we need human touch to thrive. "Yeah, I really don't like being touched. A lot of the time when my partner tries to touch me, I shout, 'Don't touch me!'" I laugh a little, as if I'm telling a funny joke. Having already told her about my abusive relationship in high school and subsequent ectopic pregnancy rupture she says, "Do you have a history of sexual abuse?" A little stunned, I say, "Well. Yes. My first boyfriend was the only truly intimate, romantic relationship I've ever had and half of it was really bad." *Really bad* feels so inadequate here, but that's exactly what it was. She pushes her fingers down my sciatica and I cringe slightly in pain.

Carmen Maria Machado use of second person pronoun in *In The Dream House* shows me what I am. I read about the way her girlfriend's anger rolls off her body like waves of steam and I remember you. My heart rate races, and I set the book aside. I can only read it in sips and swallows. Machado writes about sitting in the car for an hour after attending a wedding with her girlfriend. When the new bride walks by and sees her weeping, Machado is relieved when they catch the slight shake of her head, signaling her to walk away. And I think of all the people who were bystanders to my misery, who still are. I think, I haven't put enough abuse in this book for people to get it. But what is enough when it comes to abuse? Does the reader need to see all the minutiae? Or will the reader already know? I conjure up a scene. It's the storm in 2007 that raked the upper west coast. It shattered the windows in our small town. I keep returning to the same moments. I've written them time and time again. It is my 18th birthday weekend and the wind thrashes outside. You have me sneak out, meet you in the woods near my house. We fight and I follow you up the hillside as you storm away, onto the black tar on a steep hill road. Crying, I reach for your hand as you pull away. You turn your body to mine and spit in my face and the hurricane-force wind propels it into my face like a paint gun. In Machado's book the *you* are her, the younger self she thought she left for dead. In this book the *you* are *you*, a curse whose name I dare not speak.

While reading about complex post-traumatic stress disorder online and the four F's (fight, flight, freeze, fawn) I read a line that says that freezing types are the most likely to categorize their trauma and abuse as not being "that bad" in order to distance themselves from the event(s). I think about the linear memoir I previously wanted to write on my relationship with my first love. I remember I was going to title it *I Was Crazy Too*, as if making that distinction, that I was crazy, not because of the abuse but despite it, would give me control over what happened to me. The title and a line from an old pop song floats into my mind, "love don't cost a thing," but it turns out it does. It cost me a whole hell of a lot and ten years later I still can't retrieve it all. The memories extract, contract, extract, but they are not linear. There is nothing linear about abuse. It is a frame. Not a time frame. I can only frame snapshots, but where do they fall? What happened in between? I can't remember, but when he kissed me, I burned inside. When he cut me, didn't I bleed all over the place? My grief crawls into tight, dark places but my anger is something I refuse to replace. The world would have me forgive, move on. But tell me, how do you forgive a monster under the bed?

Her girlfriend's grip around her arm tightens, begins to hurt, causing a bruise in *In the Dream House*; I am in the green Dodge neon again in the woods. It is dark all around and inside me, and the rain keeps coming down. You grab me by the arms and shake me. *Shaken baby syndrome*, I think later. I clench my fists, turn my body, and use the strength from years of playing soccer to twist and kick you with both feet in the chest. Your body slams against the passenger door and I bolt from my car. I dead-sprint in the dead of night. A full circle from the beginning of our relationship, when I bolted from my first truck when a bee flew in the window and you had to slide over and grab the wheel and press in the brake. We laughed. No one is laughing now. Later, the prints of your fingers, temporary tattoos across my arm for weeks. I wear only hoodies so my mom will not see the purple-yellow glow.

After not speaking for a few days, we meet up. I show him the fingerprints he left on my arm. He kisses each mark lightly, a ghost of his own hand, my body a bag of nails. He is quiet. There is only an implied sorry on his face, his head drops in grief at what he can become. Later that week I change my number. I leave him for his best friend. A bruise for a bruise.

How many times can I tell the same story? Will this noise inside me ever lose its breath?

I've already written these things. Either earlier in this book or before, in essays that have appeared in random journals. I can't stop returning to the scenes. I'm being chased and hunted by my own memory. It won't let me sleep.

An elliptical, illusion, hazard zone. Do not enter the twilight zone. Do not press go.

Taxidermied Love

VII.

And who am I, hour
late, hoarding roadkill under
blankets, like softness—
gratuitous in its bland
kindness—can temper dying?

I once had a friend who said, "One day I'm going to turn you into a story and when you call, the crows will come." What I think she meant was, *I want to peck out your eyes.*

If you're searching for forgiveness, you will not find it here. These aren't the questions that plague me in the blue light of early morning. I twist my palms inwards and manifest forests in my lungs. I dreamt in fairy tale creatures and when the same crows came to call, I turned my back from them, and for this, I will never be forgiven.

I once received a phone call from a man who used to be a young blond boy who said, "Look, I know it's not right, but when she hit me I pulled her from the car by her hair, dragged her down to the ground and left her on the side of the road."

These are the questions that follow me into the night.

A friend once said, "I'll write you letters." What I think he meant is, *We've both gotten very good at being alone.*

My youngest dog sidles up next to me and leans his whole body against mine, dropping his head to rest on my chest, his forehead tucked under my chin. I place my book down and pet him, singing, "Baby Mine" by Bette Midler. The spring birds trill outside the open backdoor and the moment is overlaid by an alternative life: me rocking in a rocking chair, a baby with blond hair against my chest, my body humming the tune in the sunlight. And I think how that's a life I'll never have. And I think about picking up my phone, sending myself this fragment for my book. And I think how fortunate that I'm able to do this, that I don't, instead, have to set down a baby to write and hear its mewling cry. My dog whines a little as I pet him, then is distracted by some sweet smell or sound on the wafting air. And here I am. The crows are calling and I'm writing this fragment, phone in hand, sun warming my back through the windowpane.

In the cool February night, we took our dogs on their first walk in months. We came around the corner of the park and there was the super snow moon, bright orange looming in the sky, casting its glow on the puddles, across the field nearby where a few froggy croaks leached into the darkness. The dogs sniffed and snorted and galloped, and I remembered how much more I could love my life if I could only step into it. At some point in my illness, I became a no-man. When I'm not knocked out by fatigue or stomach aches, I'm preemptively worried about fatigue levels, nearness to a bathroom, what I will feel like the next day and the next. But how hard is it to take a five-block walk and hear the world's few remaining wild animals and watch my partner and my dogs frolic in the moonlight?

It's raining outside the car, but it feels like it is raining inside the car, inside my head. I called a therapist's office

141

that my insurance covers and left a voicemail. "Yeah, hi. My name is Shilo and I have multiple autoimmune disorders and am hoping to find a therapist that can help me manage the constant anxiety I have." Directly after leaving the message, I have an anxiety attack. Not from the call, but from the nausea and rising levels of acid reflux that have been happening all day.

Taking the trash out, I notice that the iris stalks are pushing up through the soil. Then, I notice that *A* has cleaned the dead leaves out of my flower beds and from around the base of my prickly roses.

Who said romance is dead.

A man came into my work to buy movie tickets early. I was wearing a sweater with a pigeon on it. He became animated and told me about how his father used to raise pigeons. They had pigeon coops all over their backyard. Wistfully, he looked up into a memory I could not see. "It was the happiest time of my life," he said.

At the Exquisite Creatures exhibit of Christopher Marley's art, a young boy and his father looked at the exoskeletons of seahorse. Crying, the boy asked his dad, "Why do they have no bones?" He repeated this question over and over, tears streaming down his face.

After the exhibit, after spending two hours looking at the rows of beetle bodies lined up, the butterflies' wings set in a series of kaleidoscopes, the preserved iguanas, fish, various bugs, flora and fauna, spending the most time in front of the various birds, wings tucked or splayed, a line from *The Notebook* repeats in my head, "If you're a bird, I'm a bird." We're driving down the street while the rain pours. A couple stands at the bus stop, lip-locked in vigor, rigor, rigor- mortis. I keep seeing the birds, frozen in time, beaks tucked into their bodies. An eternal sleep. And I don't think about kissing my partner in the rain. We laugh at the couple, and he says, "Yesterday at the DMV a couple was making out right next to the counter where I was filling out my paperwork. They just wouldn't stop." *Just.* And we laugh again. But yesterday was Valentine's Day and when he mentioned sex I said, "I resent the expectation of sex for holidays," but what I was really thinking was, *we just spent the day at the cancer facility for our oldest dog and all I want to do is hold her close to my body, just breath her in, just don't touch me, just don't.* And we did not do it and he snored for an hour next to me and the dogs before I woke him and told him to roll over. And he said, "I haven't been snoring. I haven't been asleep." Thinking no time had passed at all, an hour of our dog's life gone by. And we're driving down the road on our valentine's do-over and the rain continues to fall. I spot spring flowers blossoming all around the Pacific Northwest world and in my head a teal bird, its wings tucked, its head dipped in permanent prayer.

But I'm ahead of myself, or behind. While walking through the exhibit, he knew the name of almost every animal, fish, insect, crustacean, snake, lizard, bird, bug. "How do you know that?" I asked, bewildered, "How do you know?"

At bedtime he moves over slowly to my side of the bed. It's been months. I still don't feel ready. I try to get into it, for his sake. Living with me is so unfair. My body won't respond the way I want it to, the way I need it to. His stocky body towers over mine. "I'm sorry," I repeat, again and again as he tries to caress me tenderly. I can't get out of my head. I can't retrieve the moment. Near tears I say, "Let me try something." I get up, lean over his body. I'm still not there, but I no longer feel like crying. I needed to take the power back, bring it back to my body. I give him what he needs but take nothing. He is a kind man and something inside me feels broken in this moment. I do not know if I can get it back.

I brought one of my best friends to my hometown on the coast. Sitting in the sun at a park looking out at the river she said, "I can't wait to see the ocean. My friend told me to say hello to our mother when I see her. She speaks French and told me that the words for ocean and mother are the same."

We go to the spot where I carved my initials when I was young. They are still brutally deep, cut into the wood. Sometime in the last couple years someone carved a heart above them. Its tip ends at the top of the N in my name, attached. When I return to the places of my youth, I look for the three first, middle, and last initials of my first loves name. He used to write and carve them everywhere. I do not find them anywhere, as if he came back through and erased himself from all of our spots. Like a dream, a nightmare, a figment I created on the page. Maybe they are hidden from me, my eye no longer trained to gravitate toward his lines.

Driving down a backroad an old memory shimmers like a mirage in the distance. I'm being yelled at to pull the car over. When I do, you pull the keys from the ignition, start walking away from me and chuck the keys onto the hillside in the blackberry brambles. The rain is coming down in sheets and I'm crying. I search the brambles for what feels like hours, cuts all over my hands, see you walking back down the highway toward me. You find the keys within five minutes, walk me back to the car, pretend that nothing happened as we drive away. Then I'm back in my Jeep, the sun is shining and one of my best friends sits next to me, another friend drives in the car ahead. We pull up to the waterfall, follow the trail down to the water, stand at the base, our faces coated in mist from fifteen feet away.

Sitting on the torso of a giant cedarwood that's been felled by a storm I ask the friend who still lives there, "Do you experience moments here that have memory superimposed over them? Whenever I come to visit it's like a reel of film is playing over whatever I am doing, wherever I go. Maybe it is different for you, since you live here?" We stare into the trees for a long while and I think about how on the drive here. I had a clear memory play out in my head that happened during an area we drove by where my ex threw my keys into the blackberry brambles. From the silence she says, "I wish so many of your memories here weren't bad ones of Voldemort." Unfortunately, I was with him most of the time I lived here. More time than I wasn't. But they aren't all bad. For instance, every time I drive between Peter Pan Market and the old cemetery that he lived by I see myself running through the dark of the night, ducking behind cars or bushes when I saw headlights, sprinting to his house to sneak in and have sex. Now that was a good time.

Our oldest dog is covered in lumps. Later this week, I'll take her back to the cancer specialist so they can do spot-mapping. The process of identifying all the spots of concern and marking them on a dog-shaped chart. The giant lump on her chest has gotten bigger. It protrudes when she stands. *A* says I'm just paranoid, that it hasn't gotten any bigger, but I know denial when I see it. I've been more tender than ever with her. I try to keep her body in proximity while I'm home, give extra-long belly rubs. Notice the way she snorts in protest, licks her toes, smells like Fritos on her feet. While curled up in the nook of her neck this morning, I kiss her chest where the lump is. *Maybe true love will make this go away.* I breathe in the salty scent of her.

Each extra day I get looking into her joyful, joyful face is a little less sorrowful.

I dreamt I moved into an apartment with a woman who had to flee her life. Running away from a man, no doubt, as we all must do at one time or another. For some of us, we are always running. The women filled her hallway and doorjamb with nails, rusty and jutting out at all angles to stop the predator. I took a broom to the nails and swept them out into the sunshine. I won't be needing these, dream-self said as she swept, but behind me the TV played a static station, loud and crackling in the background. Outside, my dog sat tethered to a tree, watching.

I dreamt that my old undergrad creative writing teacher got mauled by a bear and used a carrot peeler to make clay chalk to create hieroglyphs under the bridge where he was attacked. Later, when he wandered off on his own wedding day, I said, "You know how he is. He will reappear and start telling us how he got lost in a 2000-page book about Kafka's musing on butterflies."

I dreamt there was an A-frame cabin sitting at the top of a mountain between two peaks. I dreamt that my ex-boyfriend was there. The snow blocked the way out of the door, but I wasn't scared to be trapped there. He was in the shower, and I walked into the bathroom. He grabbed me around the hips through the shower curtain and I could feel the contour of my body fit his. Suddenly, I was naked and there was no shower curtain, just our bodies under the steaming water. We fell against a wall where someone was sleeping on the other side. *Shh*, he laughed as he brushed the hair out of my face, cupped my cheeks and tilted my lips toward his. It was a dream, but these moments were not dreaming. When he wasn't manic or raging, he treated my body with tenderness.

I woke feeling stunted by the day. As if, before dawn fully rose, something had been taken from me.

I want to be tough. It's unfortunate that being seen comes with such a lofty price.

I want to be unforgettable like that, want to steal someone's dreams from under their own feet.

In a dream *A* wrote: It's okay that your love comes in waves.

A is in the ironworker's apprenticeship program, working twelve-hour days, with an hour commute both ways, seven days a week. He is awake for an hour after he gets home. We have shared two chaste kisses in the last few weeks.

On social media Maurice Carlos Ruffin wrote, "If you see an attractive person in a café, do not approach them. Instead, go home, wash your hands, and write a sad, yearning poem."

I had a dream that *A* drove us over a bridge in the dark to an old chapel where his whole family was waiting. They plan to force me to marry him. I grab our oldest dog who is the size of a tiny pup and run away in the night with her. The road turns into Young's Bay and I'm forced to climb the walls with the dog in my hand. I slip into the water and the dog drowns. I resuscitate her with CPR. When I arrive at his parent's house, which is also the apartment I shared with my second serious boyfriend, my other dog is there to greet us. *A* arrives and it's like the whole wedding debacle never happened. A momentary fever of insanity.

We haven't had winter in Portland, but yesterday at the grocery store, I turn the corner to the exit door and see that giant snowflakes careen to the ground. "Holy shit" I stop in my tracks. A lady walking behind me shrugs, eyes wide, and we laugh for a moment, holding up the exit line.

We fall asleep with Ragnar between our bodies, as we do every night, but *A*'s hand is resting on my hip. I wake up hours later, my pajamas, where his hand has been, is covered in sweat, our bodies a solitary lake.

In the prologue of *Birds, Art, Life*, by Kyo Maclear, she writes about anticipatory grief, which is a lot like anticipatory anxiety, from my experiences. The anxiety, the grief, comes not from the actual experience of the loss, but from the imagined version of it. We are practicing our grief like a child who puts on a cape. We know it is not real, at least not yet, but it billows out and around us, tainting everything all the same.

When fear looms around you, you start stacking the deck. Let me live long enough to finish the *Big Bang Theory*. To watch this hummingbird collect pollen from the pink flowers growing through the fence. To smell the lilacs in bloom, watch the cherry blossoms outside my bedroom window unfold. Let me live long enough to finish my book, to get it accepted, to see it in print. To finish my degree, to watch my parents grow old, to watch my niece and nephew grow old, to grow old. Let me be there when my dogs pass from old age, to learn to love again—properly without barriers and expectations of a letdown—to renovate the kitchen, to sell this house and buy a house somewhere quiet, to have sex again at a time when I want to have sex and can connect two bodies, to walk in the woods, to write a ghost story and another ghost story and another. Until, until, until.

A peer from my undergrad who only recently broke up with her boyfriend a month or so ago writes a poem about how his lack of reaching out had made her realize, more than anything, that the love they had is dead. All I can think is, what if the other person is also thinking, I was waiting for you to call and you never did, so I, too, now think our love is truly dead.

If you die, I will not be fine. I imagine myself crying on the caskets of everyone I've ever loved, whether I want them in my life or wish them apart from me always. I'd never wish for someone to not be in the world, to not breathe in sweet clean air. I imagine my ex-lovers crying quietly, in private, bodies tucked in. I imagine A in our home, alone with the dogs and his quiet and steady grief, pacing the halls.

While thinking about birds I remembered stopping at the bottle-drop one day. A took the bags full of cans and bottles in while I waited in the car. As time continued to pass, I grew antsy. Where was he? What was taking so long? When he finally came back to the car I said, "What the fuck?" He told me he had seen a bunch of people gathered around a vehicle, crouched on the ground. Thinking they were having vehicle trouble he went over to help. They were trying to coax a terrified pigeon out from under the vehicle whose legs were pinned together by fishing string. It couldn't walk. He went over, laid down on the tar, cupped the bird and pulled it out from under the car. He held it while someone else clipped the string and then he set the bird free.

Every sunny day we've had, I sit out on the lounge chair with a book in my lap. Most of the time I'm not reading. Every time I do read, up the armrest comes creeping a curious black and white jumping spider. It is the largest jumping spider I've ever seen. "Excuse me," I say, waving my book near it. The spider retreats under the chair until I open my book again.

It is the second day of spring. Birds sing their twittering songs. The smell of smoke and the crackle of fire drift to me from two houses over. I watch two robins fight each other for something in the plum tree. Tonight, when it gets dark and the stars come out, the frogs will croak in the distance and *A* will be home for one short hour where we can talk about the stupidity of human ego and laugh at reruns of a television show before he goes to sleep early and I lay awake in our bed filled with crushing desire.

Fortunes abound today. A downy woodpecker landed in my maple tree and tap, tap, tapped its way into my heart.

I dreamt that I was a tall blond actress that I've seen on TV. In the dream I was married to a tall male actor, but I was having an affair with a long-haired man who was full of Hijinx and we were nearly caught multiple times by my husband. When I awoke from the dream, I felt lighthearted for a moment.

I dreamt that it was summer. I was walking back from a nearby Mexican restaurant wearing a pair of overalls and a crop top. The warm summer breeze blew through my hair. People were outside all around, getting on and off the bus, walking from the grocery store. A group of school aged children road their bikes down the sidewalk. I came across a basket with two baby alpacas inside it. Before that, I dreamed I was playing soccer again. In the dream I had forgotten soccer was something I used to play. I lay in the grass on the side of the field, running my fingers through the long green strands, waiting to get subbed in.

I told my therapist of the dreams over our virtual appointment. "What do you think those dreams were trying to tell you?" She asked. "To have hope," I say, "to imagine joy."

Taxidermied Love

VIII.

Taxidermied love
never seemed cruel / a stuffed fox
can't bite / but oh / teeth
gleam from his mantle / I stick
my finger in all the same.

Images by Rachel Lauren Photography

I receive a letter from a dear poet-friend. *I am determined to not fill my letters with talk of what we are all fearing*—she writes. I take her letter into the backyard, sit down on the wooden bench during the momentary reprieve from the rainstorms, another wave which is brewing on the periphery of the western sky. Instead, she writes to me of her garden, of all the planting her and her husband have been doing.

At the end she leaves me with a poem by Ada Limon called *Homesick.*

Take some time to imagine yourself as a strong and sheltering tree and be at piece my friend, she writes.

I look up into the maple, imaging a tree in my heart.

As we crawl into bed I reach for *A*, place my cold hand on his spine.

I spend most of my days piecing together puzzles. At night, as the anxiety that's been hunkering down like a wolf in the bush rises up, I close my eyes and see puzzle pieces, my mind trying to fit together its imaginary protective bubble. If I could just get this one piece to fit this next piece and the next and the next. At best, it's a latch on an invisible door.

It is overcast with bouts of rain. My anxiety is skyrocketing, so I put on my souled moccasins, take my peppermint tea and book of poetry, and go sit outside. The sun comes out and Roxy, our oldest dog, climbs up on the picnic table, lays down like the statue of Anubis, head held high. I imagine her saying, "Ahha! A sliver of sunlight. I must catch it!"

I come into the house because the sky has turned a twirling grey and looks like it's about to open up. The light pouring into our bedroom is dim, hazy. I curl up in our bed next to a book of poems I've been carrying around. I hit a joint one, two, three times before putting it out. Roxy snoots around the edge of the bed, circling. I can't lift her up and *A* is not here to do it. Nor is he here to see me laying on our bed and try to get bedroom things going, so I can't snuggle her and I can't giggle and resist him and my old dog stares me in the eye and makes a perfect 'O' shape with her mouth and begins to bark.

I keep thinking about a dream I had years ago. In it I was on the coast and the sky churned grey, then deep purple, and the ocean rose almighty and powerful and overtook the humans and their buildings, all of us at once. People were ripped out to sea, vehicles, houses, the building all around me. All that stood through the storm was a white Grecian

157

pillar, and me, with my arms wrapped tightly around it. The water thrashed but I didn't let go.

I can't stop thinking about the dead dog alongside the highway in Wyoming. For weeks every time we drove by it or my sister and I walked by it on the way to get malt chocolate ice cream from the gas station, I turned to look at it, even though I didn't want to. I couldn't stop myself. I watched it slowly, day by day, decay and decomposition. The fur sank into its ribs. Eventually that's all it was. Pearly white ribs jutting out of the desert into the clear blue sky.

I imagine elaborate scenes of meeting new girlfriends and becoming fast friends, sitting out by the fire in the evening laughing, laying down in the grass and staring up at the tops of trees. It seems I am always in search of a connection that I feel I have somehow missed out on, despite my numerous girlfriends I have currently, who I would and have undoubtedly done these things with. But then I realize that what I am fantasizing about isn't platonic. It's the world of same-gendered relationships that I have only almost experienced and have to forfeit in order to stay in the life I've already created.

In *Greedy: Notes From A Bisexual Who Wants Too Much*, Jen Winston writes about never feeling queer enough, feeling outside of the queer community inside her multisexual label. Maybe that's what I'm building here, my own queer community, populated with my lovers: imagined, ghosted, almost, never-enoughs and otherwise.

I keep my fantasy of living in the movie *Fried Green Tomatoes* alive by wearing overalls and burying my repressed sexuality in these pages.

I wake in the middle of the night and find my body curled near *A*'s, our elbows touching.

I use an earlier edited draft of this book to help start fires in the firepit out back. One piece of paper has the line, "It seems that all I have left is control." I take a video of it beginning to burn. Hours later I find a small piece of the paper left, what is left on the scrap is, "It seems that all I have left." I trace my fingers over the edges, post a picture of it online. A friend says, "It's like a little poem island."

We spend the next weekend in the sunshine doing yard work, have a barbeque in the evening and laugh about inconsequential things.

I notice the cherry blossom tree spent the day unfurling pink, delicate flowers. Elated I stand directly underneath its branches and turn my face up.

I dream that my first love is waiting outside a thrift shop I work at in a car with a dog. He asks if he can take me to the river, take me fishing. He looks good. *I've been clean nine months and I live in a small town, so small there is only one street. Didn't you always want to live with me and a dog in a small town with one street?* He says. He casts a line out into the river and a group of girls sit on the shore giggling and when I look up, it's like the sky has been turned into a landscape of stars.

My therapist asks, "What is it you need from him in this moment?" I say, "He can't actually give me what I need right now. I need to heal. He isn't the one who hurt me. It's out of his hands."

All this time I haven't been paying close enough attention. How could I not see what we were doing together, building a life? And yet I still didn't know. I still don't know. Is the life that I build with this man the one I always wanted? *What am I to do with all this unused desire?*

In a short story, a character of Amber Sparks asks that no one share their boring dreams. But again and again I'm compelled to come here. I need someone to know about this double-speak, double-life, cheating on my waking life with this terrifying and exciting and vibrant and cruel other life. I don't confess out of guilt or shame. I carry none of that here. What use do I have, already nearly died twice, for your judgements? Life is too short and mine is likely shorter. That's why I get to live it twice. There is no shame, only this gnawing sense that the teeth of my second life are biting into the hard, frozen soil under the feet of my waking life.

I dreamt, I was on a pirate ship and one of my ex-boyfriends was the captain. We had to go to battle against another magical, flying ship. There was a tree in the center of the ship and when I touched it, everything, the ship, all the humans, turned to ice and the tree under my hand was a crystallized wonder.

Last night I dreamt of someone I could have fallen in love with. I was in Arizona, just passing through. I took a video of the sunset on my phone, the most spectacular pinks and oranges, the tan of the desert turning black, the lines blurring in the coming dark. I tried to send them the video from my phone, but the message wouldn't load. I woke feeling unfilled with their name pressed into the grooves in the top of my mouth, the pressure swollen like the pain after eating a slice of pineapple.

I dreamt that my niece's rabbit got out and I spent hours searching for it only to have it jump into my hands scrambling to outrun something, invisible to me, chasing it.

I dreamt that a beautiful woman was dancing and singing to me, as if she were a siren. By the time I got to her, I was weak with desire and woke mid orgasm.

In "A New Theory for Why We Dream", written by Taylor McNeil about the dream science theories of Erik Hoel, she writes about how dreams may very well be a survival tactic." Maybe that's what I've been doing all along. Learning to survive in this body of illness, in this body of loneliness and grief and desire and starving ravishing hunger.

After I cheat on my partner in a dream last night, his own best friend comes down the river walk and speaks with me. "You are starving for soul connection," he says. When I begin crying in the dream, it starts raining and the water sizzles on the black tar of the street when it lands, turning to a foggy mist all around. When I look up, I am alone in a parking lot on the edge of the Columbia River, crying on my knees.

I often feel like the people I dream of are dreaming of me at the same time. I especially think this is true of those I've loved deeply. In our waking lives, wherever those may be, the string between our bodies is loose and winding, but when we dream of one another, the string gets tighter, pulled taut between us as if we could locate the tether and traverse the balance beam to reach out and clasp hands. We are still connected despite my greatest daylight efforts to the contrary.

We spend a warm, May day doing yard work. I garden, gather wood into stacks from the trimmed down trees, split succulents from pots cracked by winter ice storms into other pots, and then sit by the firepit reading a ghost story. *A* rakes and mows, pressure washes the patio and takes apart wooden patio furniture his dad built out of pallet boards that has started rotting from the years spent in the rain. He burns one chair, piece by piece. While he is pressure washing, I take another chair, tip it upside-down on the firepit, and watch the flames lick up the back, devouring the chair in one swallow. Mesmerized, I say to him, "Look, look!" He appears baffled, asks why I did it that way. "Because I wanted to watch how it burns." When the back has disintegrated, I take pictures of the charred ends, a frame looking out into the bright green world. Over my shoulder, the light pink petals of the cherry blossom drift to the ground in the breeze.

At the grocery store, *A* rests his head on my shoulder in the cracker aisle. In a dream, an old love crying, buries his head in my lap. In bed, *A* runs his hand down the side of my back, my hip. "What do you think you are doing," I say. "Loving you," he responds.

Each night I rest my head between my dogs, opposite of my partner, they each fall asleep, one by one, before me. The other night in his sleep, *A* said, "That's what this dude is doing. He's thinking about how I was out here picking up snails and cats, months and months ago." I am so tickled by this sleep thought, that I can't sleep for a while after. The absurd nature of his dream, so wholesome in its nature, strikes me as such a good reason for love. Meanwhile, in my sleep, I am a generator of desire, throttling against my own yearnings. Meanwhile, my chosen love collects, and no doubt nurtures, the world's wild creatures in his sleep.

I won't apologize for writing you green letters, won't make amends for the creep of lime, the lace-patchwork lattice hanging from the vines. I am forested, rain-soaked, because I learned about hunger in the darkened woods, learned what it means to be ravished, to be ravishing. Is it my fault if you haven't felt the thick shag of moss between your fingers, toes, dimpling your body, a bed for bare bottoms? With over twelve thousand species of moss can't you see, look at me, am I not fern, spring, seaweed, pine, venom, clover, frog, mint, pistachio, jungle, lime-lime-lime green? Don't I cling to what in me is dead, what is dying, which is me, after all, which is you? And aren't I bright and shining, holy fucking alive and hunter, sage, tea, emerald, mossy mellow, glistening with the morning dew?

Reading Playlist

1. *Wedlocked* by Jay Ponteri
2. *300 Arguments* by Sarah Manguso
3. *Girlfriends, Ghosts, and Other Stories* by Robert Walser
4. *Women Hollering Creek* by Sandra Cisneros
5. *The God of Small Things* by Arundhati Roy
6. *Love Poems* by Pablo Neruda
7. Every book ever written by Alice Hoffman
8. *A Thousand Mornings* by Mary Oliver
9. *Eternal on the Water* by Joseph Monninger
10. *The Sexual Life of Catherine M.* by Catherine Millet
11. *Unmastered* by Katherine Angel
12. *Knock Wood* by Jennifer Militello
13. *Poems 1968-1972* by Denise Levertov
14. *My Love is a Dead Arctic Explorer* by Paige Ackerson-Kiely
15. *Mink River* by Brian Doyle
16. *Thirst* by Mary Oliver
17. *Sweet Dreams, Story Catcher* by Brian Doyle
18. *The Seas* by Samantha Hunt
19. *The Folded Clock: A Diary* by Heidi Julavits
20. *Motherhood* by Sheila Heti
21. *Sylvia* by Leonard Michaels
22. *The Taiga Syndrome* by Cristina Rivera Garza
23. *Gephyromania* by T.C. Tolbert
24. *The Dream House* by Carmen Maria Machado
25. *Birds, Art, Life* by Kyo Maclear
26. *Greedy: Notes From A Bisexual Who Wants Too Much* by Jen Winston
27. *And I Do Not Forgive You* by Amber Sparks

Thank You, Thank You, Thank You's

To my first reader, Catherine Kyle, whose eyes were the first to see any of these pages and who encouraged me to keep writing it when the vulnerability seemed too much. Other first readers, mentors, and workshoppers include Sarah Manguso, Tim Horvath, David Ryan, Jennifer Militello, the entire New England College MFA squad, with special thanks to Crystal, Lee, Reverie, and Nichole, and all the others who sometimes didn't understand what the hell I was trying to do but were supportive in the space between the fragments. Second readers and dear dear-hearts, Delilah Martinez (who appears in these pages many times), Becky Lauer, Jack Eikrem, and Joe Ballard, whose friendships got me through undergrad. Mentor, friend, and blurber, Jay Ponteri, for showing me the myriad ways that creative nonfiction can appear on the page and the way that white space can act as ghost, grief, trauma, illness, body, home, and love. To my best-best friends—some already listed above, you know who you are—whose unrelenting love and laughter I am eternally grateful for: Jordana Grabenhorst, Andrea Gonzalez, Ani Franz, Brittany Sumpter (also the best sister a girl could ask for), and Derek Turner. To Emmi Greer from Buckman Publishing who spent two hours on zoom with me helping me find an ending for this book that wasn't consumed by the pandemic, which had overtaken the initial draft of this monster in the last 30 pages. Major, unending adoration and thanks to Emily Perkovich, publisher, editor, graphic cover designer extraordinaire from Querencia Press and her press partner Savannah Verdin for caring for this book and giving it a home, but also for making a small press that gives indie authors and poets the care and love their books deserve. If you are a writer reading this, this is your hint to submit your book! To my parents and A's parents for your unwavering love and support, even when I told you what the book is about, and especially for agreeing to buy but not read it! You are the real MVP's. To my large extended family for always being my biggest cheerleaders, with special thank you to my little brother Dustin for writing terrible lyrics with me that summer we lived in Texas together. And finally, to my partner of almost 11 years. It hasn't been easy for you, being in a relationship with someone with loads of chronic illness, trauma, baggage, and a lot of anger for the things that have been done to their body and the continual ways their body has betrayed them. We are turning 33 this year, so officially a third of our lives has been spent together, and you take everything in stride. Thanks for making me laugh, for all the inside jokes, for your support in all aspects of life, even when you don't understand why I feel compelled to do things. Thanks for giving me a cozy home I can fill with books and a backyard where I can lounge in my hammock and watch our dogs run around. Thanks, mostly, for your kind heart.